UnaLIENable

What It *Really* Means and Why It Matters

Your Rights, Our Stories, and America's Survival

DR. THOMAS V. GIORDANO

**Copyright © 2020 by G.E.T. Management, LLC.
All Rights Reserved.**

No part of this publication may be reproduced, distributed, or transmitted in any form or by any means, including photocopying, recording, or other electronic or mechanical methods, or by any information storage and retrieval system without the prior written permission of the publisher, except in the case of very brief quotations embodied in critical reviews and certain other noncommercial uses permitted by copyright law.

Edited by Katelyn VerSprill, Ph.D.
Cover design by Laeeq Hussain Arif

ISBN: 978-1-7357415-0-5

DEDICATION

This book is dedicated to my children, Chrystal and Cecilia, to my nieces and nephews, Donna, Gregory, Nicole, Carla and Little Marco and to all of the generations to follow.

He who controls the school controls the grammar. He who controls the grammar controls the discourse!

Dr. Thomas V. Giordano

unaLIENable quiz

To test your knowledge of the basic principles discussed in this book, go to –

www.ProLibertyForum.com/Unalienable-Quiz

You will also receive a free subscription to the ProLibertyForum Newsletter and future Podcasts

CONTENTS

Introduction
Chapter 1: Just Who Was Buster, Anyway?   1
Chapter 2: The Basis of Buster's Views   19

PART I - LIBERTY

Chapter 3: Buster on Liberty   33
Chapter 4: More on Liberty   45
Chapter 5: La Manu Niura   57
Chapter 6: Natural Liberty   65

PART II - GOVERNMENT

Chapter 7: Just What is Government, Anyway?   73
Chapter 8: Anarchy   85
Chapter 9: How Government Creates an Environment for Organized Crime   101
Chapter 10: It Was Just Applied Wrong   111
Chapter 11: The Socialist in the Classroom   137

PART III – ECONOMICS

Chapter 12: Human Desire, Human Choice, Human Action	167
Chapter 13: What is Money, Dad?	175
Chapter 14: Economics Explained	187
Chapter 15: The Waters of Gravelly Run	197
Chapter 16: The Longhorn Battalion	211
Chapter 17: Friedman's Four Ways of Spending Money	219
Chapter 18: Why Things Go Bust	227
Chapter 19: The Minimum Wage	237
Chapter 20: Another Classroom, Another Socialist	249
Epilogue	271

INTRODUCTION

A man nicknamed *Buster* showed me that I was either unintentionally misinformed or lied to outright. I understood that I was not alone. In fact, practically everyone to whom I've ever spoken, when asked what that simple word in the title means, gave me the wrong definition or a synonym that, when examined, was way off base. I also found that the word was almost universally mispronounced! Buster also showed me that that simple word, *properly* pronounced and defined, was the very foundation of what makes the United States of America exceptional; why it is the greatest governmental experiment in human history.

The first question I would expect a prospective reader of this book to ask is: "Who is this '*Buster*' fellow and why should I be interested in what he had to say?"

Buster was my father, Mario John Giordano. He was endowed with a special insight into matters of liberty, government and economics which he freely shared. His unique perception came from his personal experiences. Over the course of his life, he went from a street-smart kid and high school drop-out from South Philadelphia to a World War Veteran to a *G.I. Bill* success story with multiple university degrees to an educator, entrepreneur, practical philosopher, and sage.

In order to appreciate his perspective on life, I believe that a brief history of our family is necessary to disclose the mold from which he was cast. I trust this would be a telling indication of his world view and, as such, I will dedicate the first chapter to span the time from our family's arrival on the shores of the United States through his formal education, and on through some of his professional accomplishments. My father's formal education, though extensive, really only furnished him the tools he needed to research the questions his experiences generated and the knowledge he sought. It was his informal education that provided most of the answers he wanted.

My father was blessed with an exceptional intelligence and was as much a student as he was a teacher all of his adult life. His areas of expertise were education, business administration and economics, but his passions were for history and philosophy and he was able to link all of these subjects with a rare clarity.

His views on liberty, government and economics were based upon simple truths and concepts of voluntary interaction between people for their mutual benefit. He had no doubts that our rights, liberty included, are our birthright which no governmental power had any authority to either grant or deny and that they are not subject to commerce. He saw it as a mistaken belief that government had the authority to do to society what we as a people would consider criminal if done by an individual or a group of individuals to another. He abhorred coercion and the use of force or the threat of harm used by one party to force their will upon another and, as such, found no positive value to society in any political philosophy based upon the involuntary commandeering and redistribution of another's private property. By "*private property*" he intended a person's body, their time, their intellectual productivity, their physical labor, their wealth, their possessions, their real estate, and their liberty.

Though he was by no means an anarchist, he was a believer in the maxim "***the government that governs best governs least.***" He was neither a democrat nor a republican and he would have described himself as a classic liberal in the tradition of Thomas Jefferson, whom he greatly admired. He was enthusiastic about the concepts espoused by the Founding Fathers of the United States and was saddened by the steady deterioration of their principles by our ever-expanding, over-intrusive government and the resultant degradation of our society.

He lamented the gradual slippage into socialism and the usurpation of state and individual rights by a federal government that creates laws to which it is not subject, that presumes ownership of our property, our wealth, our time, our labor and our person, and that, necessarily, creates three classes of people – taxpayers, tax consumers and the intermediaries between them.

In the sphere of economics, he was an adherent of the

Austrian School and had very little time for the *Marxian* or the *Keynesian* models, which he had studied in depth and considered irrational, unoriginal, arrogant in their presumptuousness and destructive to society. He favored *Free Enterprise*, the *Free Market Economy*, *Private Capitalism*, *sound money* and was contrary to the very existence of the *Federal Reserve System*.

As was implied above, he was of that generation forged in the Great Depression, tempered in the brutal bloodbath of World War II and honed by the experience that comes with age and reason. He attempted to communicate his insights to me by using my own personal experiences growing up, as object lessons. Some of these are what I hope to illustrate upon the following pages. He also counseled several of my cousins and many of his colleagues and students at our dining room table over a cup of coffee. His instruction has guided my brothers and me and many others throughout our lives.

So, **why should the prospective reader be interested in my father's insights?** Because you may also benefit from knowing that ***you*** too have been either unintentionally misinformed or lied to outright. Buster's life was well examined and well spent. He answered any questions posed to him with a sincere clarity. He also had a positive effect upon the majority of those he came in contact with but angered many who saw his honest and truthful observations as a threat to their dogma.

I have divided this work into three separate parts – Liberty, Government, and Economics. My father

UNALIENABLE

believed that all of these should be intertwined by a common strand - people pursuing their individual interests and desires in the absence of coercion. These lessons will be presented by order of subject, not by order of chronology.

T.V.G.

CHAPTER 1

JUST WHO WAS BUSTER, ANYWAY?

Mario John Giordano was born in 1925 in the *City of Philadelphia* to an Italian immigrant father and an American-born mother of Italian descent. He was the youngest of four sons. The *casata* to which he was born was of an ancient and noble family from the *City of Lanciano* in the province of *Chieti*, in the region of *Abruzzo, Italy*. Both his father and grandfather, however, were born in the town of *Fossacesia*, some 18 kilometers to the east of Lanciano on the Adriatic coast.

His grandfather, Don Carlo Alberto Giordano, preceded the rest of his family by two years, arriving at Ellis Island on the 27th of September, 1907 aboard the *RMS Campania*, a ship of the Cunard Line. He was not part of the mass of immigrants from southern Italy escaping poverty and misery to seek a new life in America; he was sent by the *Banco di Roma* to set up a bank branch in Philadelphia as a conduit to facilitate the money transfers of immigrants back to their native country.

Don Carlo was so impressed by the vigor, the absence of government bureaucracy and the opportunities of the American free market economy, that he immediately jumped into business, reproducing what the family had done for centuries in Abruzzo. Over the course of the next two years, he purchased thirty homes in south Philadelphia and turned them into rental properties for which there was a high demand amongst the recent arrivals and upwardly climbing immigrants. In 1909, the rest of the family arrived, including the then thirteen-year-old Don Nicola, my grandfather.

The family's fortunes progressed steadily all the way through the teens and into the twenties. My grandfather trained as a tailor along with his younger brother, Don Francesco, and they opened a shop on the corner of 13th and Tasker Streets in south Philadelphia. Don Nicola had an international, immigrant workforce of five master tailors and the operation was successful, serving the upper echelon of Philadelphia's political, professional and civil societies. The word of the quality of his work eventually brought in patrons from the tri-state area and beyond. Even a governor of Pennsylvania had the *Giordano Tailors* label in his suits.

The family's good fortune in the New World, however, started to take an abrupt turn in 1921, when Don Francesco, then twenty-one, was gunned down while sitting at his sewing machine after an argument with a co-worker. This would be the first misfortune to befall the family since its arrival in America, but it would not be the last. Two years later, my grandparents lost their third child, *Carmela*, to influenza. She was only six months of age. My uncle Nick and my father were born in the two years following Carmela's death. The most devastating tragedy to hit the family, however, came in 1929 when my grandmother, Maria, passed away at the age of twenty-nine to kidney failure following an infection. At the time of her death, my father was just under four years of age.

On Tuesday, the 29th of October of that same year, the stock market crashed and the Great Depression gradually followed. Eventually, one third of the banks closed their doors and one third of the currency was sequestered out of circulation. As a consequence, Don Carlo lost everything he had accrued with the exception of his own home. Don Nicola's business was hit hard, but was still operational and profitable. Even so, because he was a single parent with four young children, he had difficulties taking care of the boys while running his business. He eventually went to the Catholic Church and arranged to have them placed under foster care until such time as his circumstances would allow him to provide a more stable home.

The two older boys wound up in good, sound environments, one on a farm and one in a professional's household. My uncle Nick and my father, however, were assigned to a working-class, Irish family. My grandfather visited the boys once a week without fail. My father once told me that he watched my grandfather bow his head and weep into his handkerchief minutes after leaving from one of his visits. He was completely unaware of the treatment his children were receiving with this foster family until one day when he arrived unannounced and immediately understood that his boys were being maltreated and abused. My grandfather left the home that very moment with his two children and had to make different arrangements.

My father and his brother were now separated. Again, my father found himself with another working-class, Irish family, this time with eight children of their own. Here, however, he found a loving family whose mother was very kind and compassionate. He would spend the next three and a half years with them in comfort, but was still happy when it was time to be re-united with his father and three brothers.

My father was able to return home at the age of seven after my grandfather wed for the second time. He and his brothers were relatively well-adjusted after their experiences, but my father had an air of sadness about him and he never smiled. Because of his dead-pan expression, his brothers gave him the nickname "***Buster***" after the comedic film actor Buster Keaton. His stepmother didn't care much for him and he felt it and kept his distance.

Because of my grandfather's success at tailoring, the boys were always well-dressed and better off than most, even during the darkest days of the Depression, but they were not immune to its effects on the others in their neighborhood. The streets were unforgiving and they all grew up tough, street-smart and able to defend themselves.

From the time they returned home, all of the boys helped out in the shop and became quite good at tailoring themselves, but this was not what my grandfather wanted for them, as he valued a formal education above everything else. He rarely spoke of the privileged life the family led in Abruzzo, but sometimes reminisced about the family's ancestral palazzo in Lanciano and a villa his great-grandfather had built on the *Lago di Bomba*. Of course, his sons thought he was exaggerating and didn't really believe him.

On December 7th, 1941, the Imperial Japanese Navy attacked the U.S. Naval base at Pearl Harbor in the Hawaiian Islands. The United States was now at war with the Empire of Japan. Within days, Germany and Italy declared war on the United States. My Uncles Frank and Nick enlisted in the U.S. Army soon afterwards where one was trained as an artillery forward observer and the other as a fighter pilot for the U.S. Army Air Corps. Although he tried every branch of the Armed Services, my uncle Carl, the eldest of the four brothers, was considered unfit for duty due to a congenital kidney defect. He would sit out the war stateside. My father finished the 10th grade and, in July of 1942, went to work at Gimbel's Department Store in Philadelphia. In June of 1943, my father turned eighteen and left Gimbel's to join the U.S. Navy.

After boot camp at Camp Peary, on the north side of the Virginia Peninsula in York County, Virginia, he was assigned to the 123rd United States Naval Construction Battalion where he did training at Port Hueneme, California. He was then sent to Hawaii.

What happened next would have a profound effect upon my father's psyche, one that would be a major drive in his search for knowledge, understanding, and truth.

In January of 1944, my father was gearing up to head to the Midway Island with his battalion when he was called to his Commanding Officer's office. Upon reporting, he was handed a Red Cross telegram. My grandfather had died of a heart attack at forty-seven years of age. In the chaos around the battalion's preparations for deployment, the telegram was delivered to my father a week late and he had already missed the funeral. He was given liberty to return to Philadelphia. During the three-day trip across the continent to the city, the train stopped in Chicago and my father de-boarded to stretch his legs and buy a newspaper. The paper reported that the transport ship carrying the 123rd was struck by an enemy torpedo, decimating his battalion. He was absolutely convinced that his father had died to get him off of that ship and save his life.

Returning to duty upon his arrival from Philadelphia, he was re-assigned to the 39th Sea Bees which was attached to the 2nd Marine Division. Though it is difficult – practically insulting – to summarize a man's experiences in war, suffice it to say that my father engaged in seventeen battles in the Marshall and Marianas Islands Campaign over the next two years. He was wounded twice by shrapnel from Japanese bombs and took a bullet from a Japanese Zero aboard a destroyer during transport. He also contracted malaria and "jungle rot," a fungal infection of his feet. These would stay with him as constant reminders of the South Pacific for the rest of his life.

Soon after Saipan, Tinian and Rota were secured, my father's unit was temporarily detached from their base on Saipan and assigned to take part in building an airstrip on the Island of Tinian. Though he had no idea of the importance of what he was witnessing, he watched from afar the departure of the Enola Gay on its secret mission to Hiroshima. Nagasaki followed and, when the Pacific War ended, he headed stateside from Saipan. He was discharged from the service in March of 1946.

He was not yet twenty-one years old and had some decisions to make. He hadn't finished high school; both of his parents were dead and there was no one waiting for him at home. His strained relationship with his stepmother excluded any desire to remain with her. By then, my uncle Carl had gotten married and was living with his wife in the Harrisburg area. My uncle Nick had been released from the Army Air Corps and had already returned to the city from the south Pacific. My uncle Frank, however, was still in Germany with the Army of Occupation, after having fought in General George Patton's Third Army across France, Belgium and into Bavaria. My father contacted his eldest brother and went to Harrisburg from San Francisco.

He found his brother was having some financial difficulties, so he offered to help and my uncle Carl offered him a place to stay. I cannot be sure of my father's mental state after his release from the service, but I do know that one day he shot off a clip of rifle rounds through my aunt's open kitchen door without even thinking. This frightened the daylights out of my aunt Kay and my uncle Carl suggested to my father that it was time for him to go. After some consideration, he decided to return to San Francisco, but wanted first to see his brother Nick and some other relatives in Philadelphia to inform them of his decision.

The first person my father looked for when he got to Philadelphia was my uncle Nick. He had assumed that his brother had gone home, but not even he had returned to his father's house. My step-grandmother told my father that his brother's friend, Vince Melso, convinced his parents to let Nick stay with them until he got on his feet. Vince's parents were immigrants from *Terranova da Sibari* in the province of *Cosenza*, in the region of *Calabria, Italy*. Their home was located on the corner of Dickenson and Wilder Streets near 12th Street, only a few blocks away from Giordano's Tailor Shop which had ceased operations some two years earlier. When my father rang the Melso's doorbell, Vince's younger sister, Concetta, answered the door. At the sight of this young woman, he immediately decided to forget about California and remained in the city. A year later, they were married.

To support himself, my father got a job in a container factory making boxes. One day, while on a lunch break, he looked around and realized he didn't belong there. He was sure he wanted to fulfill his father's wishes for a formal education, but was impeded by the fact that he hadn't yet finished high school. Since there was no way of getting around it, he found another option that, at the time, didn't require a high school diploma for enrollment.

He decided to apply to the National Optical School to become a licensed optician. It was a one-year course which he attended from 1946 to 1947. At the time he completed his schooling, the field was dominated by only two providers of equipment and lenses – American Optical and Bausch & Lomb. He wanted to set up shop in Philadelphia, but these companies had policies that prevented him from opening up in competition with others selling their products and he was told that if he didn't open a shop where they referred him, they would not provide him with the machinery and primary materials to operate. He was told there was an opportunity in up-state Pennsylvania. My mother didn't want to move out of the city, so my father told her that if that was what she really wanted, he would return to school and she would have to support that decision by going to work. For the next two years, he worked in various places doing various jobs until both of them finally agreed that it was time to get serious about getting a higher education. It was then that my father, at the age of twenty-three in the Spring of 1949, enrolled in the 11th grade at Temple University High School to begin his studies for a diploma. Imagine, if you will, the sight of a twenty-three-year-old, battle-hardened veteran sitting in class with a group of sixteen- and seventeen-year-olds. Needless to say, because of his maturity and determination, he excelled in the accelerated program and graduated with honors in November of that same year.

To support themselves, my mother worked as a bank teller and my father was hired as a maximum-security guard at the Moyamensing Prison where he worked full-time on the graveyard shift. He was accepted to Temple University and, aided by the G.I. Bill, went as a full-time student during the day. It was at Temple that he encountered real prejudice for the first time.

There was a particular professor named Polischuk who made no bones about his disdain for returning veterans using the G.I. Bill to attend school or about expressing an outright hatred for Italians. On the first day of his class, he asked the veterans to identify themselves by raising their hands. Afterwards, he told them that they didn't belong in institutions of higher learning and they probably wouldn't make it past the first semester. His opinion of Italians was equally disdainful. As far as he was concerned, they were better suited to being shot dead in the streets of south Philly by their own criminal element. This man was smack dab in the middle of my father's curriculum and would pose a continuing obstacle as the next four years progressed. To cite one example, my father wrote a thesis for one of Polischuk's classes on the comparison of the industrial and agrarian economies of the North and South during the Civil War. He earned a "C" for the paper. A year later, he gave the paper to a Jewish friend who was taking the same class. Although Polischuk was also anti-Semitic, my father's friend's last name was Miller and his religious background was not apparent. Mr. Miller changed only the coversheet and received an "A" for the same paper and was praised by Polischuk for the superb quality of the research, presentation and conclusions.

He also met opposition at the prison.

Some three years into his degree program, his Commanding Officer at Moyamensing informed my father of an examination for promotion. My father told him that he was not interested in the promotion and was happy doing what he was doing. My father had a fixed routine and was able to study between rounds all through the night. He had set up a chair and table on the top tier and found it very conducive to study once the inmates were locked down and the lights were out. His superior retaliated and placed pressure on him because of his refusal. Policies were drawn up aimed directly at my father's studying that forbid guards from entering the cell blocks with books of any kind. For his remaining year, my father's way around this was to take a razorblade and slice the chapters from the texts he was studying and sneak them into work in his lunch bag.

When my father was about to graduate with honors with his *Bachelor of Science in Education*, Polischuk learned that he was working while going to school. He petitioned the faculty to deny my father the diploma on the grounds that, by his working a full-time job, he had demeaned the degree. When the other faculty members reviewed his grades and realized that the only average grades he had received were from the petitioner and that, despite them, he was still to graduate with honors, they denied the request. However, to appease Polischuk, my father's name and picture would be omitted from those of the graduating class in the university yearbook. Of all of the returning veterans who started with my father, he was the only one to make it through.

In 1960, it would be Polischuk who was to hand my father the diploma for his *Master's in Business Education*, also with honors, at the graduation ceremony. My father neither shook his hand nor thanked him. He simply took the diploma and walked away.

He started his teaching career at Overbrook Regional Senior High School in Lindenwold, Camden County, New Jersey within months of being awarded his undergraduate degree from Temple University in 1954. He was tested all of his life and at every turn and his first day at Overbrook was no different.

My father told me what transpired in his homeroom class on his first day. Being a new teacher, some of the students were seeing how far they could push him. They had no idea just whom it was they were pushing.

One student sitting in the back of the class, whom my father described as a "jack-booted tough guy wearing a leather motorcycle jacket," pulled out a switch-blade stiletto and started cleaning under his fingernails. He was silently daring my father to do something. He closed his roll book and walked to the back of the room and confronted the young man. My father put out his hand

and ordered him to hand over the knife, to which the student replied that he'd have to take it from him.

My father told him," Look, I was raised in the toughest neighborhood in south Philly. I fought two years in the south Pacific before I was twenty-one and I worked my way through college as a maximum-security prison guard at Moyamensing. Do you think a snot-nosed punk like you is going to scare me with that pig-sticker?"

Within milliseconds, my father had taken the knife, grabbed the boy by his hair and lifted the stunned student out of his seat. He then walked him tip-toed to the door and down the hallway to the principal's office as the other students poured out of the classroom behind them to watch. He opened the door to the principal's office, kicked the boy into the anteroom and placed the knife on the counter. The principal came running out of his office when he heard the commotion.

"What are you doing, Mario!?" he yelled.

"He pulled a knife on me; he's not to return to my class again!" was my father's response.

From that first day, no one challenged my father again and the school had finally found the right teacher to handle their problem students. He was successful at turning them around and, by example, showing them the importance of an education. Once my father realized that these kids had never been taught how to study, he devised a systematic approach to the matter and instructed his students on his methods. Their grades improved measurably and the administration, as well as the parents, were impressed with his results.

DR. THOMAS V. GIORDANO

During the course of his tenure at Overbrook, a colleague named Al Rossi convinced him to get his M.Ed. to open up more opportunities. My father took his advice and worked as a teacher during the day while taking his graduate classes at night at Temple University. As previously mentioned, he graduated in 1960 with honors. While at Overbrook, he developed an idea for giving high school students a work-study experience. This idea was referred to as *Distributive Education*. Its aim was to provide the students about to enter the work force with enough trade skills as incentives for future employers.

He remained at Overbrook until 1964 when he was named Assistant to the Superintendent of the Gloucester Township School District, Camden County, New Jersey.

In 1966, he was approached by agents of the Radio Corporation of America to develop an educational system for teaching the computer languages FORTRAN and COBOL to fulfill the need for more programmers in the government, military and business communities. He took the job and had to pour into the study of these languages to gain the expertise needed to compile a new teaching method. He became an Educational Systems Designer and Proposals Administrator for RCA and immediately began the grant proposal process for government sponsorship. He was successful at his efforts; the grant was awarded and the work began to standardize these languages for teaching purposes. His abilities did not go unrecognized by some agencies of the federal government and he soon began evaluating proposals sent to the Department of Labor, the Department of Health, Education and Welfare, the Office of Emergency Communications, the Peace Corps, and the Bureau of Indian Affairs, among others. Additionally, he became such an expert in the computer languages that he was asked to contribute his expertise to the refinements of the computer programming for the AEGIS Combat System which was then being developed by the Missile and Surface Radar Division at RCA.

His methods worked out so well that the upper management approached him with another project – the development of an educational system to teach the people of Micronesia to construct electronic equipment for RCA. The corporation viewed this as doubly important because it was developing a less costly labor force and, by the same token, increasing the standard of living for the Micronesians. It meant, however, that my father's presence was essential for its implementation and that he and our family would be required to move to the South Pacific for a minimum of two years. It also meant that my father was being groomed for an Executive Vice President position at the company.

My mother objected again to moving so far away and my father declined the opportunity. He did, however, design the system and handed it over to a colleague at the corporation to implement. He knew that his refusal had effectively shut down any chance for promotion into an upper management position, so in 1968, he put in his application to return to teaching at the college level at the newly formed Camden County College in Blackwood,

New Jersey. He was accepted to the position, resigned from RCA and would spend the rest of his teaching career as a professor and as Chairman of their Business Department, where he taught Business Administration, Secretarial Sciences and Economics. He was also placed in charge of the college's night school and developed a program called Junior Business Training – JBT. This, too, was based upon concepts similar to the distributive education model he had developed for the trades at Overbrook.

In 1969, my father joined forces with Dr. John D. Stewart, II – a professor of History at the college – to design the nation's first formal Afro-American Civilization course for the United Planning Organization in Washington, D.C. The six-week course was created for the federal government's Concentrated Employment Program, which was co-sponsored by the Departments of Labor and Health, Education and Welfare to provide African Americans with jobs as well as an appreciation of their heritage and the contributions of Black Americans to U.S. history.

In the 1970s, he was determined to develop an educational system based upon the individual needs and capabilities of students. He had always pondered the single-most important problem with the government's educational system and how to overcome it. He was keenly aware that the progress of classroom activities was as fast as the slowest person in the room and that the pace of the educational process was based upon that. This was detrimental to the average and quicker students and left them bored and distracted while the teachers concentrated on the needs of their slower classmates. He devised a method of dividing each subject into pertinent facts in small doses – called modules - to be studied and tested. Once a module was completed and the student was tested and passed with 100% retention of the material, they would pass to the next module and so on until the course was completed.

There were several advantages to this approach; the first being that the student proceeded at their own intellectual pace. The second was that once students had passed a given module, they could test other students working on the modules that they had already completed. The third was that more material could be covered and mastered than the traditional *10-10* rule (only 10% of any given subject can truly be presented and only on 10% of that can students actually be tested.). The fourth advantage was that everyone who completed the course effectively had a grade of 100%, practically eliminating the traditional grading system which was based as much upon the subjectivity of the instructor as it was upon the objectivity of written test and assignment scores. This may also have been an effective way for future students to avoid having to confront a Polischuk in their path.

He wrote up a proposal for this model, which he named the Non-Lock-Step Educational System or NLSES and was awarded a grant by the federal government to develop and test it. The report on his developmental progress was published and showed so much promise that several universities that critiqued it were enthusiastic about the concept. The University of Miami contacted my father, stating that they would use the proposal and report as a doctoral thesis and award him a Ph.D. in Education if he were to come down to Florida and implement the program there. My father declined the offer, but told them he would act as an advisor, should they need him.

When all was said and done, my father had actually found a position that gave him precisely what he was looking for – time to pursue his personal interests and studies. His schedule basically had him at the college from 8:00 to 11:30 a.m. during the week and he was generally home by noon. He could dedicate the rest of the day to a small printing business and the study of philosophy, which he considered fundamental to business, economics, liberty and government.

My father dedicated practically all of his home time to study, occasionally posing questions to me and giving me instruction on the concepts he was studying. This was usually done at the kitchen table over a cup of coffee. Sometimes, the topics of discussion came up over a current event, sometimes over an experience. These discourses started from the time I was about eight until well into my thirties. Because of these sessions, I came to realize that my own formal education was based upon lies, half-truths, and omissions and that what one believes to be the truth is often unexamined and a reflection of someone else's conclusions or propaganda.

My father retired from teaching in 1988. On December 18, 1993, he passed from this life at the age of sixty-eight from metastatic cancer. My younger brother, Gary, held his hand as he died with Frank Sinatra's *My Way* playing in the background.

CHAPTER 2

THE BASIS OF BUSTER'S VIEWS

At the time of my father's death in December of 1993, my mother found herself with hundreds of his books, binders of hand-written notes and boxes of tape-recordings of his class lectures. After a while, my mother's impulse was to throw this accumulation of his belongings away, but my brothers and I insisted that it be left alone until we had the time to sort through it and possibly organize it. He had a tendency to write his personal notes and observations in the margins of the texts as he read, so there was an opportunity to see his thinking process as he was absorbing the content. As of the writing of this book, I still haven't had the time to complete this task.

The breadth and depth of his curiosity was reflected in the titles, the authors and the subject matter of the books in his library. Also, there were the ever-present dictionaries, both the general and the specific to a given body of knowledge he was reading – he never passed a word or a phrase he didn't fully understand.

Interestingly, he had his own system for organizing his books, one not based upon anything like the *Dewey Decimal System*. It was based upon general themes, such as philosophy, theology, economics, history, politics and government. His library was organized chronologically within these various subjects. For example, if I asked him a question about the meaning of an expression, such as "*good money after bad*", he could reference the statement from Gresham to Smythe to Copernicus to d'Oresme and all the way back to Aristophanes.

His books were his repository of knowledge to which he referred, but his basic view on the human condition was simple and direct. One of my earliest glimpses into my father's thoughts on the nature of man's existence occurred when I was twelve-years-old.

My father was raised a Roman Catholic. As such, his first exposure to philosophy was theological. In his younger years, he never appreciated neither the role of the church in the spreading of knowledge and western civilization nor its importance to philosophy and science in general.

One Saturday morning in the summer of 1968, I came into the house after mowing the lawn to find my father in his recliner reading a copy of Chesterton's *Saint Thomas Aquinas - The Dumb Ox*. His concentration while reading was unshakable. I passed him without saying a word and went upstairs to shower. When I returned some twenty minutes later, I told him I was going to make some lunch and asked if he wanted a potato omelet. He nodded and I told him I'd call him when it was ready.

As we sat down to eat, he asked me if I had ever heard of Saint Thomas Aquinas and I replied that I had, but knew little about him. Of course, at twelve years of age, I really couldn't have been expected to know much about Saint Thomas as questions of theology and philosophy were not a priority to me then. He told me that he started pondering the nature of things on a train ride from Chicago to Philadelphia after his father had died. All through the war, he witnessed death, misery, and destruction. While he initially participated willingly to defend our country, the "cause" faded very quickly. It became more of a struggle for survival and an obligation to protect the mates around him from harm. In any case, any academic pursuit for understanding was delayed by the war. His instructions were replaced by simple observations of human action under extreme circumstances.

He said that, for him, the starting point for his inquiries was Saint Thomas, as it was he who set down the five proofs of the existence of God the Creator. This was an essential basis of a long chain of reasoning for what he sought. In other words, he accepted the existence of a *Prime Mover* and *Efficient Cause* based upon Saint Thomas' logical and rational arguments rather than those based merely upon faith.

My father's position was that God was, is, and always will be, the purest act of existence itself in which and through which all things exist. It was God who put the universe in motion and was the first actual cause of every other action and reaction that follows. He postulated that these were the sources of the immutable cosmic and natural laws that govern everything and everyone. This was the playing field upon which man was placed; it has boundaries, rules, regulations, goals and penalties.

On the question of man, my father synthesized the answer in a way that I could understand. He told me that our religion tells us that man was created in the image and the likeness of God and that the meanings of "image" and "likeness" were different in the original Hebrew. The former represented the spiritual existence of man and the latter, the physical aspects of man. In other words, God created man's spirit first and then gave him form. God's goal was not only to create a servant, but one who voluntarily served, not one that was an unthinking drone. In order to act voluntarily, man was given an intellect and the ability to reason, but was imperfect by virtue of his inherent nature; perfection is only reserved for God. The ability to reason made His creation aware of choices which could only have meaning if man were imperfect and fallible, for if all choices lead to a positive result, the choice becomes meaningless and so does its process. If man's existence were to have meaning, it must necessarily be based upon "free will" or "Liberum Arbitrium" – he must be free to choose. He must be free to make mistakes and he must be free to learn from those mistakes. Personal wisdom is best gained from direct experience.

UNALIENABLE

It was from this perspective that my father explained to me that people are their own sovereigns with unconditional rights given to them by their Creator. He held that individuals were born with these rights in order to act and think freely to express their free will, to pursue their own interests, realize their own desires and potentials, and fulfill their own needs and ambitions. He further stated that groups of individuals such as families, clans, bands, tribes, and societies created codes of conduct which permitted the exercise of those rights without conflicting with others' rights within those same groups. This is where the concepts of "morality" and "ethics" were born. These codes, ideally, were voluntarily accepted and set in place to safeguard the group from the excesses of individual members for the protection and survival of the group itself. An individual's *excesses* are known by many different names depending upon which group is involved: among them are sins, transgressions, heresies, misdemeanors, crimes, felonies and treason. These codes and the reasoning behind them were then used as a basis of written laws. An example he gave was *The Ten Commandments*, which stand as a contractual agreement with God delineating how we are to worship Him and co-exist amongst ourselves. In an ideal world, man-made laws should be based upon equity, fairness, and reason and should be measurable by and against a mutually agreed upon standard.

He told me that even *Cicero* wrote that the human ability to reason enables us to recognize the principles of justice and that justice gives us law and that every valid law must be affixed to nature. Any law which is not anchored in nature is not a valid law at all.

By then, we were finishing our lunch and, as I started to clean up and prepare a pot of coffee, I posed some questions for my father.

"I understand what you're telling me and it makes sense, but there are people who don't believe in God."

He responded by saying while this was true and they have that choice, believing or not believing in God really isn't the issue. He explained that much of the Catholic doctrine is from a revision and re-introduction of the ancient Greek philosophers Plato and Aristotle. He described how Saint Thomas was of the Aristotelian school of thought whereas Saint Augustine was a proponent of Plato's views and that Saint Bonaventure seems to have proposed a combination of the two schools.

He furthered, "Obviously, neither of these two Greeks were Christians, yet they realized that there is a natural order to the universe which must be obeyed. Just whom or what put all of this into motion is really secondary to the fact that it all actually exists and how we, as rational beings, are to respond to our environment."

He continued saying that even if one believes that we are the present product of 13 billion years of gradual evolution from the beginning of the universe, or just the 4.5 billion from the birth of the planet, then we as individuals deserve those rights simply by being born of that natural process. It is the fact that we are sentient, aware of being aware and sensitive to our own individuality that gives us our humanity. The codes of morality and ethics still apply, whether God is in the picture or not. However, regardless of what one believes as far as our coming into existence, it is more a question of personal sovereignty: ***do you own your life?***

My father suggested that we do, in fact, own our own lives and everything that our lives produce. We own our intellect and our reason. We own our bodies. We own our labor and what it produces, including the production of wealth. We own what our wealth can purchase.

He clarified, "Do you think that atheists would argue that they hold no claim to themselves and were born to be murdered at will, to be enslaved or to have their property stolen at the whim of another? Let me put it to you another way; if you believe, as I do, that God gave you your rights and free will, what king, what prince, what judge or committee or commissar or any other person can force their will upon you? Who on this earth has any moral authority that equals or surpasses the Creator's to coerce you to do something against your will? The atheists may believe what they wish, as long as they don't insist that I accept that my rights come from a government or some other source that goes to the bathroom the same as I do."

The first thing that came to my mind was the police. After the assassination of Dr. King in April, riots sprung up everywhere. Cities like Washington and Chicago looked like war zones and the police reacted with extreme force.

"Okay," he responded, "let's think about that for a moment. Do you have the right to protect or defend yourself as an individual?"

I said," Yes, I do."

"Does society have a right, being a collection of individuals, to protect or defend itself?"

"I'd say it does."

"There is your answer; you defend yourself with your fists or a weapon and society defends itself through a government with a police force or an army and a navy. The only time force is justifiable is for the protection of life, property or an individual's or a group's rights," he said, "and the same thing can be said for war; it is only justifiable if it is defensive, not aggressive."

"You have to make the distinction, "he continued," between society and government, Tommy; they are not the same thing. Most of the ills of society are caused by wrong-headed government policies. The disenfranchised, in their frustration, lash out at society rather than the source of their problems. Regardless of this, the point is that individual sovereignty is the actual starting point and center of our civil, economic and political existences and the rules that apply to one should apply to all. Also, when you consider that everything you produce is a direct result of your choices based upon expressing your free will, who has the right to take away, by force, anything that belongs to you?"

"The government runs on tax money. If you don't pay, they'll come after you and take it," I asserted.

"Tommy, taxation, as it has become, is little more than

legalized plunder and pure theft," He replied." It is the first immorality of government. However, there are a few legitimate reasons for taxes."

I asked him, "What do you mean by *'legitimate?'*"

"Well, in a free society, the role of government is precisely defined by its constitution, which is actually a contract between the People and the government. It is simply a commercial charter. If the government is to act within its bounds, it really has only one, primary goal – to secure the citizens' liberties and their lives. This is accomplished by three functions: the first is to wage war against foreign aggression; the second is to maintain the peace internally, the third is to maintain a level playing field for commerce. Taxes should only be levied for the things that the People have agreed upon and which are spelled out in the constitution. It is when the government takes your money and uses it for purposes outside the government's legitimate authority that the problems begin and taxation becomes theft."

He then said, "So let me now ask you a few questions. Suppose I come up to you on the street and put a gun to your head and order you to give me your money. Nobody would deny that robbing you with the threat of violence is an immoral act. Now, suppose I do the same thing and tell you I want to give the money to another person who is in need. No matter what '*good*' I *intend* to do with the stolen money, that act of taking it against your will renders the entire transaction immoral. Now, let's say the person who orders you to give them your money is from the IRS; is there no threat to your liberty or your property if you don't submit? Is there any material difference in morality whether you're robbed by an individual thief or a government bureaucrat?

If, on the other hand, I approach you on the street and tell you that there is someone who is in need and ask if you could contribute, voluntarily, to aiding them, you'd have a choice. You could say "*yes*" and you could decide how much you want to give or simply "*no*". Do you see the difference? Taxation, therefore, should be handed over only to fulfill only the objectives that we voluntarily agreed upon and nothing more."

The implications he was trying to put forth were beginning to become clear to me, but I must have had a puzzled look on my face because he looked at me with a knowing smile.

He continued," Alright, to make this even clearer to you, I want you to consider a few things. You have a limited time on this earth and that time represents your life. You may do anything you wish with your time. If you decide to work during your time here, there is a direct exchange for money. This exchange doesn't represent profit – it is an *even* exchange. When a government edict tells you that you have to hand over a percentage of your earnings, it is actually telling you that you owe it a percentage of your time - that is to say, your life. In a free society, the government has absolutely no authority to *place a lien* upon your time or your life. That is servitude. We are not here to serve the government; the government is here to serve us."

He added, "You see, there are those who believe that

the government has the authority to take and re-distribute your money to support others who are supposedly in need. This is not the case! Helping people in need is the role of society, not the government. The reason it cannot be the case is very simple: our government supposedly exists by the consent of the People and we have given it a precise number of privileges to act upon in our name. If I, as an individual, have no right to enter your house and take your property, steal your money or take away your liberties, I cannot grant those privileges to a government that is acting in my name. In other words, I, as a moral man, cannot grant my government the privilege of acting immorally."

"But we all like the story of Robin Hood – he stole from the rich and gave to the poor," I responded.

"That's the socialist version of the story and, like most things socialist, it's a lie. Robin Hood actually *robbed the tax man and gave back to the poor what was stolen from them.*" he responded. "That's why we like the story."

It was clear to me, even at the age of twelve, that my father's philosophy of life was founded on two simple concepts – the moral expression of free will and the absence of coercion. He interpreted these as the basic necessity for personal liberty, economic freedom, wealth production, and the role of government in a free society. It was the meter by which he could predict whether or not any action taken by people or by governments would succeed or fail, regardless of the supposed "*good intentions*" asserted to justify the acts.

DR. THOMAS V. GIORDANO

What he told me that day would stay in my thoughts for the rest of my life. Along the way through the government school system and well into my undergraduate and graduate education, my father was there to correct the lies and omissions being taught as *"truth."* My views on government and my own liberties would only begin to take shape later in life, as I reflected upon the era of misguided social upheaval that we were witnessing in the late 1960s and early 1970s.

PART I

LIBERTY

CHAPTER 3

BUSTER ON LIBERTY

When I was in the sixth grade, I was given a social studies assignment on the meaning of "*liberty*" as it applied to the framing of the *Declaration of Independence*. I generally didn't bother my father with my homework, but in this case, the only real reference I had was my history textbook and, of course, the dictionary. I started the assignment soon after dinner on the Friday it was assigned, so I wouldn't have to spend the weekend doing it.

After several frustrating minutes of staring at my textbook, I called my father to see if he had the time to give me a hand. He came over to the dining room table, where I was seated with my materials spread out before me and stood behind me.

"What's the problem, Tommy?"

"Dad, I'm stuck; I can't even seem to get started on this assignment."

"What's the assignment?"

"I have to write something on the meaning of 'liberty' in the Declaration of Independence. When I look up the word in the glossary of my text, it just says, '*freedom.*'"

"Tommy, never define a word by its synonym. Okay, how long does it have to be?"

"Just a few paragraphs."

My father then pulled out the chair next to me, sat down and started me on the process to complete the assignment. He first told me to look up the word in the dictionary and write it down. While I did this, he read over the textbook's treatment of the *Declaration*, shaking his head the entire time.

"Whoever wrote this drivel should either be shot or, at least lose his job," he muttered, "How is a kid supposed to understand the meaning of this document without a proper background into its creation? The complete document doesn't even appear here."

I responded with a blank stare. He then got up and told me to finish the definition. He returned with two old books. One contained a complete copy of the document, along with the Articles of Confederation and the United States Constitution.

"Okay, have you written down the definition?" he asked.

"Yes," I replied.

He then asked me to read out loud what I had written.

I read aloud, "The quality or state of being free: the power to do as one pleases: freedom from physical restraint: freedom from arbitrary or despotic control: the positive enjoyment of various social, political, or economic rights and privileges: the power of choice."

I began to recite the rest of the definition, but he stopped me mid-sentence.

"Okay; you can stop there because the rest doesn't apply to your theme. We're not talking about privileges, but our birthrights as human beings, so only the first definition applies. Do you understand what you've read?"

"Yes, but of these, I think only the one that talks about being free from despotic control is the one I want," I responded.

"Not so fast. You're right, but take a little time to analyze the definition. Can you tell me in what year the Declaration was written?"

"Sure, 1776."

"Do you think that the definition we use today is the same as the definition they would have used back then?"

"I don't know. Why would the definition change?"

"Sometimes they do. I have the definition from the *Black's Law Dictionary*. Now, Black's was written about a hundred years later, but this would have been as close to the legal definition that the signers would have understood the word to mean. It reads, 'Freedom; exemption from extraneous control. The power of the will, in its moral freedom, to follow the dictates of its unrestricted choice, and to direct the external acts of the individual without restraint, coercion, or control from other persons.' Do you see the commonalities between the two definitions?"

"Yes, Dad, I do. They both refer to not being forced to follow someone else's orders, to have free choice and to do as you like."

"That's not exact, but close enough. In any case, the word refers to the individual having free will and the ability to express that free will without being forced to submit to the will of others. Do you accept this definition?"

"Yes," I responded.

"Okay, now I want you to read the first two paragraphs of the Declaration of Independence out loud."

He gave me one of the books he retrieved earlier and placed it before me, pointing to the place I should start reading. So, I began.

"In congress, July 4, 1776. The unanimous Declaration of the thirteen united States of America. When in the Course of human events, it becomes necessary for one people to dissolve the political bands which have connected them with another, and to assume among the powers of the earth, the separate and equal station to which the Laws of Nature and of Nature's God entitle them, a decent respect to the opinions of mankind requires that they should declare the causes which impel them to the separation.

"We hold these truths to be self-evident, that all men are created equal, that they are endowed by their Creator with certain unalienable Rights, that among these are Life, Liberty and the pursuit of Happiness. That to secure these rights, Governments are instituted among Men, deriving their just powers from the consent of the

UNALIENABLE

governed. That whenever any Form of Government becomes destructive of these ends, it is the Right of the People to alter or to abolish it, and to institute new Government, laying its foundation on such principles and organizing its powers in such form, as to them shall seem most likely to effect their Safety and Happiness. Prudence, indeed, will dictate that Governments long established should not be changed for light and transient causes; and accordingly, all experience hath shown, that mankind are more disposed to suffer, while evils are sufferable, than to right themselves by abolishing the forms to which they are accustomed. But when a long train of abuses and usurpations, pursuing invariably the same Object evinces a design to reduce them under absolute Despotism, it is their right, it is their duty, to throw off such Government, and to provide new Guards for their future security. Such has been the patient sufferance of these Colonies; and such is now the necessity which constrains them to alter their former Systems of Government. The history of the present King of Great Britain is a history of repeated injuries and usurpations, all having in direct object the establishment of an absolute Tyranny over these States. To prove this, let Facts be submitted to a candid world."

"Okay, now stop a minute. The rest of the document lists the actual reasons the drafters gave for seeking independence from England. You can read that later, along with the final paragraph, which is just as important as the first two. I want you to look over the first paragraph and tell me what you get out of it."

I followed his instruction and read over it again. After a few seconds of thought, I stated, "They're declaring to England and the rest of the world that the colonies are entitled, by Natural Law and by God-given rights, to be free and independent from England and that, to be respectful to the rest of the world, they are going to give their reasons."

"Very good. Now, why do you think that they cite '*Natural Law*' and '*Nature's God*' in the first paragraph?

"Because our rights come from God?"

"Yes, but there is an even more compelling argument to be made because, at that time, rights were reduced to privileges granted by the king. You see, at the time of the drafting of this document, the majority of the world powers had governments that were based upon a king or royal family having a Divine Right to head their societies. It was doubly reinforced in England because the king, since the time of Henry the Eighth, was also the head of the Church of England. In other words, the king's authority was backed and validated by the church that the king himself led. In effect, the church was saying that God gave His blessing and the right of sovereignty to an individual person to lead the government and that all privileges came from the king, as though he were a proxy between the People and God. The drafters were stating here that the same authority by which King George was recognized as the sovereign of England was now going to be used as their authority to declare independence. It was a brilliant strategy, because the sovereign authorities in all of the other European countries and the rest of the world could not argue that the colonists had no rights without putting into question their own God-given authority and religious support. When you consider that the Catholic French, Spanish and Portuguese had the same arrangement, only with the Church of Rome, the drafters were automatically creating natural allies against the British.

Then, the drafters go on to enumerate their various reasons and among them are violations of both local government and individual rights. The document clearly shifts the center of power from a government to the individual, meaning that the government has to operate by the consent of the People and should not be forced upon them to suffer without recourse. That is what they mean by "tyranny." Are you beginning to see how the concept of 'liberty' is being used?"

"Yes, I think so."

"Okay, now re-read the second paragraph and tell me what sticks out to you."

I did as he told me and noticed the most famous phrase written – "We hold these truths to be self-evident, that all men are created equal, that they are endowed by their Creator with certain unalienable Rights, that among these are Life, Liberty and the pursuit of Happiness."

"Now, Tommy, pay careful attention! What did you notice there?"

"Well, it's easy to see; everyone is equal and we have rights given by God. They only name three, but they wrote 'among these' so they really mean that there are many that they are not naming."

"Very good. We'll deal with '*equality*' another time. What about that word '*unalienable*'? What do you think that means?"

"My teacher said it means that they can't be taken away?"

He raised his eyebrows and handed me Black's dictionary and told me to look up both '*inalienable*' and '*unalienable*', and I did so and was surprised to find that there was no entry for '*inalienable*'.

"I can't find '*inalienable*' in this dictionary," I told him.

"Why do you suppose that is?" he asked

"I don't know, maybe it's not a legal word."

"Right. The word '*inalienable*' didn't exist and was not in common use at the time of the writing of the document. Now look for '*unalienable*' and read me the definition."

I found the definition and read it aloud, '*incapable of being aliened, that is sold or transferred.*'

"You see the difference in what you thought the word meant and how Black's defines it? The root word is not '*alien*' but '*lien*'. The word is properly pronounced '*un-a-LIEN-able*'. This completely changes the meaning of what you thought they wrote. Your God-given, natural rights *can* be taken away, say, if you commit a crime and are put in jail or if you agree to join the armed services – even if you become elected to political office and swear an oath. Your rights, however, **cannot be transferred or sold; they are not subject to commerce without your permission!** Do you understand the implications of what this word means?"

I just looked at him and stared back at the word in the dictionary. The deeper significance within the context of the Declaration was really lost to me. I could not have known then that this 18th century word's intent and pronunciation would be gradually and, most likely intentionally, transformed in American dictionaries around the time of the progressive administrations of Teddy Roosevelt and Woodrow Wilson.

My father continued, "Tommy, this is a very important concept that our founding fathers understood clearly. It was commonly accepted as truth and part and parcel to the British and American legal philosophy at the time these events went on. You see, our Natural Rights existed before the drafting of this document and, consequently, the Constitution. They understood the overriding laws of nature as the basis of our freedoms, to which the government could attach no claims or conditions – that is to say *liens* – and that the interests of the People are superior to those of the government. Do you understand?"

"I think I do."

I replied that I did, but it would be much later in my life that I would come to understand the core consequences of this word on the American experiment and how it is the basis of our unique American philosophy. It would become very apparent to me that the only reason for this change in meaning was to create a dishonest basis for a strawman argumentation to attack our founding principles.

"Okay. Well, I don't expect you to truly understand the significance right now, but before you start writing, I want you to look up one more word – *'independence'*.

I did so and came up with the following definition; 'the quality or state of not being under the control of, reliant on, or connected with someone or something else.'"

"So, when we're talking about liberty, are we talking about being more dependent or less dependent upon someone or something else?" my father questioned.

"Less dependent. So, the more dependent we are upon something else, like a government, the less liberty we have," I concluded.

"Right. Now you can write up your theme with a fuller knowledge of the terms and the mindset of the people who wrote the document."

My father left me to my assignment and told me he would read it when it was completed. He was satisfied with my report, but hadn't finished his lesson to me on liberty. We were now at the kitchen table and he told me to go and retrieve the book we had referenced earlier.

"You still have the last paragraph to read," he reminded me.

I returned to the kitchen and did so aloud.

"We, therefore, the Representatives of the united States of America, in General Congress, Assembled, appealing to the Supreme Judge of the world for the rectitude of our intentions, do, in the Name, and by Authority of the good People of these Colonies, solemnly publish and declare, That these United Colonies are, and of Right ought to be Free and Independent States; that they are Absolved from all Allegiance to the British Crown, and that all

political connection between them and the State of Great Britain, is and ought to be totally dissolved; and that as Free and Independent States, they have full Power to levy War, conclude Peace, contract Alliances, establish Commerce, and to do all other Acts and Things which Independent States may of right do. And for the support of this Declaration, with a firm reliance on the protection of divine Providence, we mutually pledge to each other our Lives, our Fortunes and our sacred Honor."

"There are several things that you should get out of this last paragraph," he told me. "The first is that their intentions were honest. The second is that their authority comes from the *People*, all of which are sovereign individuals equal to the King of England and the third actually gives us their understanding of the role of government in a free society. The fourth is that they refer to each, individual colony as a "state" equal to the "state" of Great Britain. Also, look at how many times the framers refer to God in the document. Don't let anyone convince you that these men were atheists or that they intended a separation of God and government – a specific religion, yes; God, no."

He went on to describe the Declaration as the "mission statement" of the federation and the Constitution as its commercial charter – that is, the government's "working papers". The structure was the same as any legal incorporation, such as Coca-Cola, U.S. Steel or General Motors.

I did come away with a clear understanding of the intent of the Declaration of Independence and of the meaning of liberty upon which our federal government would eventually be founded. But, my father had more in store for me as to the understanding of liberty and its many forms. He was not done with me, yet.

CHAPTER 4

MORE ON LIBERTY

My assignment was complete and my books and papers were put away and I could now enjoy my weekend without worry. I returned to the kitchen, where my father was still drinking his coffee.

"Thanks for the help, Dad," I said.

He looked at me and nodded his head.

"I noticed that your textbook was pretty vague on the concept of liberty; has your teacher mentioned anything about this in class?"

"Not really. She just said that the Declaration put down these principles, but the signers were slave-holders," I responded.

"Typical," he muttered, "Maybe you should ask your teacher what she was implying by this observation. Tommy, practically every civilization from the beginning of our written history had slavery in one form or another. It is only relatively recently that our Western

Civilization made a concerted effort to abolish slavery. It is still being practiced, even today. The ancients considered it a normal way of life. In fact, did you know that our own people were liberated after the slaves here in the United States? In the Kingdom of Naples, and then the Kingdom of the Two Sicilies, before the so-called "unification" of Italy, there was feudalism until the French Invasion in 1806 and, even though the French had abolished it, it remained in effect until 1892. Your mother's parents were born to serfdom, in Calabria. Our people were not free, by law, to emigrate from Italy until after that year. Ninety percent of the population could not vote. Well, England was no different than any other nation and, by default, so were the English colonies – it was the same society."

"To tell you the truth, I don't think much about slavery at all, other than to know it's wrong." I responded.

"Well, you should think about it; we're never too far away from servitude and most governments are run by people who wouldn't hesitate to subject their citizens to some kind of oppression. But you're right, it is wrong on every level - morally, economically, socially. The question is whether or not we should ignore or lessen the greatness of our past cultures simply because some men presumed they had rights over other men's labor. We are not members of those societies, nor do we have any guilt for their actions, but we can appreciate what they gave to us, including the tools and the ability to *abolish* slavery and set other men free. Do you remember that word, *'unalienable'*?"

UNALIENABLE

"Yeah."

"When your teacher told you that the founding fathers held slaves, did she also tell you that one of the original complaints for why we declared independence from England was that they had brought slavery to the colonies? This reason was scratched from the final draft out of necessity to favor the southern states whose economies relied upon slave labor, but the seed for the eventual elimination of the institution of slavery was firmly planted in our founding documents with that word *'unalienable'*. It reached a boiling point with the Civil War."

"Yeah, but there is still racism and prejudice against the colored people."

"First of all, there is racism and prejudice against you, too. You just haven't experienced it firsthand, yet. Hatred will always find an avenue of expression, whether it be based upon race, religion, national origins or how a person cracks open an egg. As long as there are differences between people, the unenlightened will pre-judge and dislike others. You will find, as you grow up, that people tend to hate in others what they dislike most about themselves. However, slavery is not racist; it is economics, Tommy. It is *the transfer of ownership of someone else's labor* that drives slavery, not skin color. The overwhelming number of examples of slavery in the past were of people of the same race enslaving their neighbors or of royalty or nobility enslaving their own people. In the case of England and its colonies in North America, the number of indentured servants, bondsmen and convicted criminals forced into labor was equal to, or greater than, the number of African slaves before the Revolutionary War. Many of these "*white slaves*" were brought here against their will by force, misrepresentations or by deceit, though most came willingly to America. In fact, some estimates show that almost half of the Europeans who emigrated to the colonies were indentured, meaning their labor was sold to someone for a given number of years before they could be set free."

"How did they come here willingly?"

"Many people from Ireland, Scotland, Holland, and Germany gave up their liberties by contractual arrangement just for the passage on the ships that brought them here. The captains of those ships would then sell their indentures or bonds to redeemers in the ports of arrival who would then either keep them or sell them in turn to others. The servant or bondsman would then be obligated to re-pay the owner of the contract with their labor over a given number of years, until they were emancipated and released from service. Even Benjamin Franklin was an indentured apprentice to his older brother in Boston before running away to Philadelphia. Can you imagine what these people's conditions were in their native countries that the only option they could see was to sell themselves into servitude just for the price of the ticket to come to America?"

"It was probably pretty bad." I reasoned

"When people are voting with their feet, it is extremely unlikely that they are emigrating to worsen their conditions. You know, Tommy, liberty has a very long and bloody history. If a person were to look at our history as a species, they would find that it is more common for people to live under tyranny and in misery than it is to be free, self-sufficient and prosperous. There wasn't even a notion of freedom until the Classical Greeks came up with it and had to invent a word to describe it – *"eleftheria"*. The Romans called it *"libertas"* and, probably because they too had a slave society, the concept of freedom was able to spread throughout their empire and to the British Isles where it eventually came into the legal system with the Magna Carta. This is a very short and loose synopsis, but the fact is that we owe a great debt to the Greeks, Romans, and British for the liberties that we were intended to enjoy today in this country. And, let's not forget our Judeo-Christian traditions."

My father paused and took a sip of his coffee as though he was trying to put some order to what he was going to say next.

"I want you to think of it this way; the Jews gave us a sense of justice. When they said, "an eye for an eye and a tooth for a tooth" what they were actually saying is that punishment for a crime should be equivalent to the crime itself. The Greeks gave us a system of logic and reason to arrive at the truth. You cannot have justice without the truth being uncovered. Of course, they gave us many other things, like democracy, mathematics, geometry, aesthetics and philosophy, but it is reason based upon compliance to Natural Laws, to my mind, that is their greatest gift to us. The Romans gave us our civil society and a sense of equality under the law. And it was the Roman Catholic Church which gave order to the universe and the ability for the sciences to flourish. It was the Church, let's say "Christianity", that promoted and spread our culture with an underlying sense of tolerance, to end up where we are today. Of course, it was a bumpy road and there are too many examples of our culture going astray, but this was the result of the ambitions of men corrupting the institutions and governments they controlled."

"Dad, I was thinking about liberty when I was writing up my report. I know that the definition spoke of free will, but I can't just do what I want. A lot of things that I want to do, I have to ask your permission. What if I want to do something and you won't let me? If I do it, you'll punish me for not obeying you."

"That's true, while I am still responsible for your actions, you have to follow my instructions. It is my responsibility to teach you the boundaries you have to abide by. I have to make sure that what you do is not destructive to yourself or harmful to anyone else. For example, I can buy you a rifle. I can teach you to use that rifle, but I can't let you go around the neighborhood with it for fear that you may harm someone. Until you can assume the responsibility for your own actions, you have to obey my decisions on what you may or may not do. You are still too young to make major decisions on your own."

"So, my freedom is limited. I don't have the liberties

that you have."

"My liberties are restricted as well. This is because I choose to live within the bounds of society and the law."

"But, Dad, when we defined liberty, the definition clearly spoke about unrestricted expression of free will…"

"Tommy, your education on free will, liberty and freedom is not yet complete; these concepts have been the subject of philosophical debate for millennia. The founding fathers were part of the Enlightenment, the age of reason. A Scotsman named John Locke summed up this long line of reasoning and the legacy set down by those wiser societies like the Greeks and Romans. For the most part, the founders accepted his views. As far as the legality of our freedoms, they based their philosophy upon the writings of *Sir William Blackstone* – probably the greatest English jurist to ever live."

He paused again to collect his thoughts.

"Listen, Tommy. There are basically four kinds of liberty to keep in mind," he continued, "natural, personal, civil and political. Natural liberty is the right which nature gives to all mankind to do as they wish with their persons and their property to achieve their own happiness, as long as they act within the limits of the laws of nature and do not abuse it to the detriment of others. Personal liberty deals with free will and being independent, as we've talked about already, but also refers to a person's unrestricted ability to move around or to go wherever they wish, as long as they are not under arrest or in prison for some crime. Obviously, you can't just walk into another's home without their permission or violate another's rights in the process. You can think of Civil liberty as natural liberty restrained by the written laws of the land. As a result, every citizen is considered to have the same liberties for the greater good of the public. Political liberty is the last kind. Many people get this wrong and confuse it with civil liberty. Think of this type as the creation of a secure environment in which the people can express their civil liberties under the constitution, the structure and the nature of their established government. The political liberty of a state is based upon those essential laws which are set up to distribute the legislative and executive powers. Political liberty is supposed to give a citizen a sense of tranquility that they are secure and have nothing to fear from other citizens or the government itself. Do you understand what I've just said?"

"I think I do," I responded, "It seems to me that there is no such thing as total liberty though. Every one that you've mentioned is restricted in some way."

"That is an excellent observation, Tommy. We are not gods; we are mortal beings and cannot escape the confines of the physical universe nor of natural laws. Okay, let's see if you've understood what I've just said. Let's say, for argument's sake, that you are dropped on a desert island in the south Pacific. What kind of liberties do you have?"

"Well, civil and political liberties won't mean much if I'm alone."

"Very good. What else?"

"My personal liberty is restricted because I can only move around the island and maybe a little bit into the ocean."

"What about your natural liberties?"

"I would say that they are almost the same as if I were home, but even those are restricted on an island. I think my goals would be different and my liberties would be redirected to other goals."

"How do you mean?"

"Well, if I'm alone on an island, happiness wouldn't be my goal. My first would be surviving and my second would be trying to find a way to get off the island."

"Very good. You see, you are still making choices and you are free to pursue those choices. You have to survive, meaning your time and energies will be directed at finding water, food and resources to aid your survival. You need to find or make a shelter, tools to build with, traps to fish with, and weapons with which to hunt or defend yourself from possible predators. Your role will have changed from a schoolboy to a hunter/gatherer."

"That might be kind of cool, Dad."

"You might like it for a while, who knows? But humans are social beings; they need to be with other people. Now, returning to liberty, suppose you can't find a way off the island and you are now settled and your survival is assured. All of a sudden, another person washes up on shore. Can you envision what changes might take place?"

I had to think about that.

"Well, to my mind, not much would change, except

now there are two people," I responded.

"Would you do all the work to aid in the survival of the other guy?"

"Maybe in the beginning, but he'd have to pull his own weight, eventually."

"Why is that?"

"Because I was there first. I did all of the work to organize my own survival and it wouldn't be fair to me if another guy lived off of my work."

"Exactly. There is a limited amount of resources, so another person's presence reduces the number of resources available to you, meaning your survival is then threatened. This means you'd have to work harder and devote more time and energy to remain at the same level of survival as before the new arrival appeared."

"I would try to get the new guy to agree to divide up the work. Maybe that way, we could both spend less time and energy than we would have if we were both alone. We could come up with some rules…"

"And what kind of liberty is that?"

"Oh! Civil liberty!" I realized.

"Very good, now you're getting it. And, since you're both agreeing to abide by a process of rulemaking and decisions on actions for your mutual benefit, couldn't that be considered a governmental act? Doesn't that mean that political liberties now come into the picture? But suppose for a moment that the new guy doesn't want to agree. What options would there be? Can you think of any?"

"Well, I suppose he could try to force me to do all the

work or I could try to force him to do all the work. Maybe he would try to kill me and take over everything I built and take my place or I could kill him and continue as I did before."

"Okay, but let's imagine that murder is not an option because both of you have a moral objection to taking another's life."

"I suppose we could agree to split the island in half and each take over the half we want."

"So, your resources would be reduced by half and you'd be in the position you mentioned before. Additionally, your personal liberty will have been cut in half, as well. However, this may be the best solution. So, he takes over one side of the island and you take over the other. Now, what happens? How long will it be before the isolation gets the best of you both?"

"I don't know."

"Well, suppose the new guy doesn't know how to fish. You would have an advantage over him and could trade your fish or some of your traps to him for something that he has that you need or want. Suppose he is better at farming or collecting water and you are better at hunting and building a shelter."

"I think that we would start to trade."

"Precisely. You've just jumped into a trade economy with all of the aspects of a market – the division of labor, the allocation of resources, and contractual obligations. The value of the goods and services would be determined by negotiations based upon the value each of you place on the good or service in its role to achieve a desired, personal goal. In economics, this is what is referred to as the 'subjective theory of value'."

"All this with just two people on an island?" I marveled.

"Yes. Now, I want you to realize that there was no person above either of you ordering the provision of those goods and services. There were just the two of you with your abilities and your needs or desires. Free will and liberty expressed lead to everything we do and have in our lives."

I realized, then, that my father was not treating me like a kid, but like a person capable of reasoning, when the proper questions were asked. He had this rare ability to get the people around him to think, but he never judged people on their inability to do so. He wasted little time, however, trying to convince people that his observations were sound. I used to think it was because he was so far above their thinking abilities, but he told me it was because he could be wrong. I never found this to be the case, even though on many occasions, I wished it were so.

CHAPTER 5

LA MANU NIURA

How one reacts to his liberties being assaulted varies from person to person. Sometimes, the only way to assure that they are maintained is to resort to violence. An honest livelihood should not be dependent upon having to pay someone for protection. It, too, should be unalienable.

It was between Christmas and New Year's Day in 1964 when all four of the Giordano brothers were together around my family's dining room table. This was a rare occasion, since my Uncle Carl and his family lived so far away in the middle of the Commonwealth of Pennsylvania. It was always exciting to see my cousins and my Aunt Kay because they were somehow different from us in the Delaware Valley. They knew practically nothing about our part of south Philly. By contrast, we still had strong ties to the old neighborhood in south Philly to where the family originally immigrated from

Abruzzo. We still went down to the Nine Street Italian Market to buy the things we couldn't find in the suburbs. We still heard the many Italian dialects and broken English spoken in the streets and understood what they were saying. My aunt was Pennsylvania Dutch and not only spoke softly but her accent seemed to me almost an Irish brogue. My four cousins, Carl, Nicky, Bobby and Mikey were all Giordanos, but I had to look hard to find the "Italian" in them. They all spoke the same way as my aunt and, at times, I didn't fully understand them. I'm sure, however, it was reciprocal.

My other cousins were closer to me and seemed more like my brothers and sisters. My Uncle Nick had one son, Little Nicky, and my Uncle Frank had two daughters – Sandy and Linda. The older cousins weren't present; they had gone somewhere with my older brother, Eddie. My little brother, Gary, who was only two years old at the time, sat in a highchair between me and our father. My mother and three aunts were in the kitchen.

One thing all of us cousins did have in common was our fascination with the experiences the four brothers had growing up in south Philly during the Depression. None of us knew either of our paternal grandparents, so listening to the four brothers reminisce gave us a little insight into who our grandparents were.

All of them had some kind of story to tell that poked fun at their father or one of their brothers. These all got a laugh out of everyone present.

My Uncle Frank then asked a question.

"Do you guys remember '*La Manu Niura*'?"

They each looked at one another with a knowing grin.

UNALIENABLE

Though the expression is properly pronounced "*La Mano Nera*" in Italian, it was more common to hear the dialectical pronunciation among the immigrants who were affected by it.

I somehow knew, by the puzzled looks on my Harrisburg cousins' faces, that they were at a loss; they knew about as much Italian as our Dutch friends across the street

I blurted out, "I know what that means – *The Black Hand!*"

"That's right, Tommy," my Uncle Frank confirmed.

My Uncle Nick started to tell the story. It happened during the 1930s when they were all teenagers. One morning, my grandfather went downstairs from their apartment to open the shop and found that someone had dipped their hand in black paint and stamped it on the wall between the front door and the display window. Everyone in the neighborhood knew the meaning of this message: it was a forewarning that you were marked, someone was going to visit you for "*protection*" money. A few days later, two well-dressed young men came to the shop.

My Uncle Carl continued the story.

"So, these two young Turks – they couldn't have been more than twenty years old - come into the shop and find Frankie at the counter. They were dressed like they just came out of a gangster movie. Nicky and Mario were not there, but I was in the shop with our father when Frankie yelled back for Pop to come out."

My Uncle Frank added," They told me in Italian to get my father. It wasn't in Sicilian; it sounded like

Calabrese…"

Uncle Carl continued, "I followed Pop out from the back. I really think he thought they were customers, until they started to talk. I couldn't make out what they were saying, until my father started to curse at them in his dialect. He got so angry that he picked up a pair of shears from the counter and went after them. As they turned to run, Pop threw the shears and hit one of them in the back. He charged them fast enough to grab one of them outside the front door and boot him in the rear end. They ran off cursing and making threats. It happened so fast that Frankie and I didn't even have a chance to get into the tussle."

One of my cousins asked," Did you call the cops?"

They all responded in chorus," *NO!*"

My father then chimed in, "There was no use calling the cops. Back then, we were all on our own, as far as this stuff went. A few days later, about three in the morning, we were all awakened to the sound of our display window being shattered. We all ran downstairs and found the glass had been broken with a brick. Pop was spitting mad and we told him to go back upstairs and all four of us slept in the shop until sunrise. We boarded up the window until we could get the glass replaced. When the two Jewish tailors showed up for work, they were frightened at the scene. Pop assured them in Yiddish that everything would be just fine and said that the shop was still open for business."

Someone asked, "…In Yiddish?"

My father continued, "Yes, in Yiddish. Your grandfather spoke five languages fluently. Don't ask me where he learned Yiddish, but that's how he communicated with the two tailors. The other three were Italian, Spanish and Irish. In any case, we picked up the brick and Frankie hid it under the counter. You see, during the early morning we came up with a plan and the brick was going to play an important role."

My father furthered, "Their retaliation was kind of weak for two guys that had their asses kicked and were humiliated in public in the middle of 13th Street. If they were really so tough, they would have done something more dramatic. You would have expected them to shoot out the window to show us that they were armed and meant business. But a brick? It sent the message we understood; they were nobodies looking to make a name for themselves."

Uncle Carl continued the story, "So, we came up with this plan. I told Nicky and Mario to try and find out where the brick came from. I thought I recognized one of the two guys, but he was older than we were and probably lived far enough away in our district that we didn't know him. Mario found the alley where the brick came from, so we figured at least one of them was familiar enough with that area that he had to live nearby. It didn't take long for us to find them both. We'd never seen them before because we found out that they were two grease balls who had recently moved to the neighborhood from Trenton. We had our marks now. To make a long story short, a couple of weeks later, we followed them on a Friday night. Mario and Frankie followed them from about a block behind and Nicky and I ahead of them, but a block over. We had to get them into a cross street so we could trap them and give them no way to escape. They finally turned left and we waited near the corner they were approaching until we saw Frankie and Mario show up at the opposite corner. Then we calmly turned the corner and walked towards them. We met them about the middle of the block and these two came running up behind. Both of the meatballs were wearing double-breasted overcoats buttoned in the lower half – this was a big mistake."

Uncle Frank went on, "Buster and I came up from behind and we each grabbed onto their collars and pulled their coats down to about their elbows. Carl spotted an alley and we dragged them both into it and started beating the living crap out of them. They were both crying and screaming in Italian. I won't say who, but one of us pulled out the brick that they used to bust the window and smashed one of them square in the face with it. The guy's nose popped like a Champaign cork and blood was spurting everywhere. Nicky pulled off one of the other guy's shoes and started clobbering his head and face with the heel. We all got our licks in. Mario was the youngest of us, but we had a tough time pulling him off of the guy he was beating on. Then, he says to them, 'We don't need protection from you; you need it from us. If any of us see either of you two within six blocks of our father's shop again, we'll kill you both. *Capite?*' Then he spits on them."

My father concluded, "We left them bloody pulps, whimpering on the ground in that alleyway. Our persuasion must have worked; we never saw nor heard from them again."

Where there was laughter before, there was a dead silence from all of the cousins now. After a pause that seemed like minutes, I asked, "Did you really mean that, Dad? Would you have killed those guys?"

He turned and looked at me squarely in the eyes, but did not answer me. However, I knew what that look meant.

My father then turned to the silent side of the table and asked, "Do you all think what we did was wrong or somehow immoral?"

There was no answer.

"Well," he said, "what we did that Friday night was as moral as it gets. My father was a businessman. He had five people working in that shop with him and each of them had families to feed. There were times when we went hungry because of his sense of obligation to pay his people before himself. Believe me, we were not wealthy, even though his business was successful. We were in the middle of the Depression and there were jackals everywhere. Two guys showing up out of nowhere and shaking us down for a percentage of my father's profits would have potentially resulted in us going hungry or one of the tailors losing his job. One sign of weakness and you were done. I've often asked myself how many other business owners in our neighborhood were saved from these two extorticnists, without even knowing it, because we didn't bow down."

He summed it up by saying, "Our liberties are constantly being threatened in one way or another. If you don't believe they are worth fighting for, then you don't understand their true value and will be the prey of every thug who wouldn't think twice about depriving you of what is yours. To my mind, it would have been immoral *not* defending our father's livelihood."

CHAPTER 6

NATURAL LIBERTY

Over the years, and through several discussions, my father made it clear to me that the government has been used as a tool in a slow but steady trend to meddle into the personal affairs of the People without ever acknowledging that its activities were in frank violation of our natural liberties. As was noted before, natural liberty is the right which nature gives to all mankind to do as they wish with their persons and their property to achieve their own happiness, as long as they act within the limits of the laws of nature and that they do not abuse it to the harm of other people. Whenever a new law was passed to *protect us from "ourselves,"* my father always commented on the foolishness of those in government who believed that there was no human activity that was beyond regulation, control or taxation. He also always questioned just who it was behind these laws and who it was that was going to profit. He saw it as the People giving up their natural rights to some authority only to then pay for permission to express them. In other words, placing a lien upon them.

I recall asking him what he thought about '*The War on Drugs*' and he remarked that it was the most stupid waste of the taxpayer's money since the *Prohibition of Alcohol*. He told me that no one ever asks if their intentions to do 'good' outweigh the harm that such wrong-headed policies cause to society. They also never seem to learn from history.

There was a time that anyone could order a pound of heroin, opium or cocaine from the Sears catalogue for a dollar and have it delivered to their door. Were there addicts? Sure, there were, but were there the high levels of crime associated with that addiction? Did little old ladies have to worry about being clubbed over the head for the loose change in their purses? Did criminal organizations sprout up to fulfill the limited demand for those drugs? No, it was just not profitable enough to bother. And just how much did those addicts cost the taxpayers?

Every time there are laws passed which prohibit human activities, people will always find a way to bypass them and the damage to society will increase. These laws also turn what would normally be law abiding citizens into criminals.

He described the general anatomy of these types of intrusions by government into the natural liberties of the People. Someone in society will either see or invent a '*social problem*' or a '*cause*' to champion, claiming that their 'cause' is in the best interests of the People. In their extreme arrogance, they believe that the People are either too immature, too child-like, or too stupid to determine what is best for themselves and need some 'parental' or 'moral' guidance. Carrie Nation, for example, claimed to be "*the Bulldog at Jesus' feet, barking at the things He doesn't like.*" The fact that Jesus drank wine didn't seem to faze this champion of prohibition. These, however, are merely smokescreens for their actual desire to force their considerations and will upon the public using the government as a club. The '*do-gooder*' will then become the '*public face*' of the effort. There will never be an outcry from the public, in general, until their cause is marketed, sold and creates a controversy. The public will then fall into the trap of taking sides and a Hegelian dialectic ensues. Interestingly, the subset of society that espouses the controls or banning of the product or the activity is never involved in the use of the said product or the activities they wish to ban.

Behind the scenes, there will be others looking for an opportunity to profit from the ban; either private citizens, business organizations, criminal enterprises or politicians looking to create a new governmental agency or police authority to enforce the new law. More often than not, the "public face" would never knowingly associate or collude with the "vested interests" looking to profit from their cause.

Politicians are then bought, cajoled or blackmailed into supporting the effort. In any other circumstance, '*campaign contributions*' to get them on board would be considered bribes and pay-offs subject to prosecution and jail time, but not with them. It is when the law is passed and enters into effect that the damage begins.

The *Volstead Act*, which was the federal law enacted to enforce the *Prohibition of Alcohol*, is a perfect example. It illustrated the unforeseen effects, both positive and negative, of the unpopular banning of the manufacture, sale and transportation of intoxicating liquors which can be readily seen.

Within the U.S., hidden stills for moonshine sprouted up in all of the major cities and in the mountain forests and woods from Virginia all the way down to Georgia. From Canada, Mexico and the Caribbean, the clandestine importation of huge amounts of liquor flowed in on boats and by vehicle to satisfy the demand. Rumrunners and bootleggers made fortunes. Bathtub gin and rot-gut whiskey could be found everywhere. Then there were the gangsters and organized crime syndicates vying for control of their geographical areas, resulting in open gang warfare, death and destruction of property. Politicians, government bureaucrats, police and judges were corrupted and bribed and the citizens became scofflaws, losing all respect for the law. This was especially true during those early depression years from 1929 until 1933 when Prohibition was finally repealed.

In south Philadelphia, as in many other neighborhoods in many other cities, the Italian immigrants ignored the law completely and continued to make home-made wines and liquors in their basements. There wasn't even an attempt to mask the sweet smells of the fermenting process wafting out of the basement windows. One of the loop holes in the law was that alcohol could be prescribed by doctors for *'medicinal'* use. Many physicians supplemented their incomes by writing scripts, filled by obliging local pharmacies. Speak-easies and private saloons were the worst-kept secrets in practically every city and town. In effect, a large, very profitable, underground industry was born in the manufacture, distribution and provision of hard drink.

On the other side of the equation was the federal enforcement of the law. Bureaucracies were created to organize their forces, control the investigations and execute enforcement. Agents were hired and paid for out of the taxes levied on the very people who were violating the law. The agents themselves were not beyond reproach and many turned a blind eye to the activities that were going on right under their noses. Even they were known to have a drink or two after their shifts had ended. Many were unwilling to risk their lives to enforce a law that even they, in their hearts, opposed.

Additionally, without real safety controls on the production of alcohol, many people became ill or died from drinking badly produced spirits.

On the positive side, many, many people gained employment during the early depression years, albeit *"illegally"*. It was probably the automobile industry that gained the most from this immoral law. People used their ingenuity to get their cars to go faster, improve engine performance and suspensions in an attempt to outrun their pursuers. These modifications found their way into the production cars and, eventually, led to the creation of NASCAR.

My father could always tell when a proposed law was a bad idea. He basically used only two criteria. The first he repeated from Frèdéric Bastiat – any law that takes something from one group against their will and gives it to another is immoral on its face. This, he viewed, as a form of the ratified, legalized plunder of the producers in a society. The second was that any law that was passed to protect the People from themselves, against their natural liberties, was doomed to fail, though not without damage to society and a high economic cost. He viewed this as "*placing a lien*" upon a natural or personal liberty and then having the audacity to charge a fee, a tax, or a system of licensure to express what was unconditionally yours in the first place.

Special interest groups, through government, have absolutely no business telling the People what they may or may not do with their own bodies. If a person wishes to smoke marijuana, shoot heroin or drink a shot glass of whisky, whose business is it but their own? Why should their liberties be taken away for an activity that hurts no one but themselves? Even if one would claim that they are harming their own families, how would their families be better off if they were in jail? Why should this mass of money and resources be dedicated to preventing people from doing what they wish? Additionally, why should the taxpayers, in general, bear any cost in interfering with individuals who wish to engage in self-destructive activities?

He would say that it is always better to calculate the harm to society against the benefits before enacting such laws. Also, it is always better to err on the side of liberty than government regulation. He once told me that the simplest, most effective way to reduce crime is to get rid of the laws which violate the free expressions of our natural liberties.

PART II

GOVERNMENT

CHAPTER 7

JUST WHAT IS GOVERNMENT, ANYWAY?

Not more than a week after I had written my report on liberty and the *Declaration of Independence*, I caught the flu and had to stay home from school. By about ten o'clock I was bored enough to get up and make myself a cup of tea. My mother was cleaning and my little brother was playing on the living room floor in front of the TV. I took my tea back to my bedroom and drank it while gazing out the window, which I had opened to get some fresh air. A few minutes had passed when my father appeared at the door.

"How are you feeling, Tommy?" he asked.

"Much better, I'm all achy but my sniffles are gone," I replied," What are you doing home?"

"I finished a project I've been working on for the last few months and handed it over to upper management. I decided to take the rest of the day off since there was little for me to do."

"Can you do that?"

"Tommy, I don't punch a clock; I've got a salaried position at RCA. I'm given objectives to fulfill by a certain time. When I'm done with one, I start another."

"Oh."

I paused a bit and continued," Dad, I'm bored to death."

"Don't you have any homework to do?"

"Not really, just some reading."

"On what?"

"Some stuff on government."

"You mean the government that was intended for us or the government we actually have?"

I really didn't think that there was much of a difference between what the founders had in mind when they formed the federal government and what it had become. In fact, I was under the impression, at that age, that there was one nation, as it says in the "Pledge of Allegiance". All throughout my education, no one had ever brought up the *Constitution of the State of New Jersey* or the Charter of the town I was living in. I knew my father was about to clear up some huge misunderstandings that my schooling had caused in me. All of my preconceptions were about to come crashing down.

I returned to my bed and sat down at the headboard and asked," What kind of government are we supposed to have?"

My father sat on my brother's bed, faced me and began to explain the basis of governments in general and of our federal government specifically.

UNALIENABLE

"Well, to understand what our founders had in mind for us, you first have to define what a government is. At its simplest, a government is an organization that a sovereign authority uses to express its will and carry out its functions. Now, the sovereign authority may change from state to state; it may be a king, a prince, a dictator, a polit bureau or even a religious leader. In our case, the People were considered the sovereigns by our founding fathers. Do you recall some of the things that were written in the *Declaration of Independence*? The clues to what the framers thought are there for all to see. They wrote about governments deriving their powers from the consent of the governed for the purpose of securing the People's rights and that the form of the governmental organization should be such that it will most likely effect their safety and happiness."

He went on," There are really only two forms of government, no matter what they are called: one is where the *People control the government* and the other is where the *government controls the People*. Now, we have a tendency to say things like 'the government does this, the government does that', or that 'the government ordered this or that' and so on, but this is all an illusion. Governments in reality are nothing more than a legal fiction, Tommy."

"A fiction? I don't understand what you mean."

He looked at me and raised his eyebrows. Then he told me something that no one had ever explained to me. Governments don't make decisions; only people do. A government doesn't breathe, eat, or go to the bathroom.

It doesn't have children. It doesn't bleed or sweat and it doesn't hear, speak or feel. It exists as a legal entity alone; it was not born, but ratified into existence and that existence is confined to pieces of paper. Additionally, he told me that, like any other organization, it cannot exist without people.

"The *Constitution of the United States* is merely a commercial charter or compact between the original thirteen States to facilitate the expression of their common interests between themselves and with the rest of the world. Just what does the Constitution do? It declares the type of government we shall have – a constitutional republic and NOT a democracy. It defines the three branches of government – the legislative, the executive, and the judicial - and it tells this organization how the powers shall be divided among these for the purposes of checks and balances. During the *Revolutionary War*, which was a war of secession just like the *Civil War*, the colonies came up with a compact for the purpose of fighting the British crown. It was a weak agreement called *The Articles of Confederation* and had very little power to enforce its authority. This is why the opening preamble to the Constitution reads '*in order to form a more perfect union*'; that was to say, more perfect than the Articles of Confederation. However, this government was to be set up so that the People were to elect their representatives to assure that their rights were not infringed upon. The several *States' Assemblies*, also elected by the People, were to *select* their Senators to safeguard their State's sovereignty from a centralization of power, and the president was to be elected by an electoral college so that the sparsely populated states would not be at a disadvantage to those more populated when electing the Chief Executive."

"The way they saw it was that each individual State was to be free and independent from the others. Each had its own constitution and each was superior to the federal government, which was considered a foreign government at the state level. Now you can understand why the federal government was designed to have no police authority, why the framers were extremely leery of it having a standing army and navy, and why, along with the printing of money, a central bank wasn't permitted."

"I didn't know all that."

"There are many things people don't know about the sensibilities of the founders. They had first-hand experience of what tyranny meant and a strong distrust of governments. The first ten amendments to the Constitution were a sign of this distrust. You've heard of the 'Bill of Rights', haven't you?"

"Yes. I don't know them all; we haven't studied them, yet."

"Well, there were some who wanted to assure that our rights, which existed before the drafting of the Constitution, were *guaranteed to never be transferred to government* and placed under controls, conditions or regulation. You see, Tommy, a *law* is a *rule for action*. When these articles say Congress "shall pass no law," they are saying that *no rules for action* or *conditions* shall be placed upon the expression of the People's rights. Can you see that our rights could be turned into *'privileges'* subject to the control of some authority? In fact, the entire government was *designed to have no rights at all*; it was only conceded sixteen privileges to act upon in our name. Also, the government cannot assume it has rights which we have not given it and anything not expressly enumerated was reserved for the States and the People. *Our government was designed to serve us, not to rule over us."*

He paused a moment and gave me an analogy," Imagine that our family had the need for a butler. Your mother and I decide that we were too busy to occupy ourselves with the daily maintenance of our home, so we put an ad in the paper offering a job. Several people answer the ad and come with their references and, deciding which is the best choice, we hire one of them. We write up a contract indicating what the duties and responsibilities are for the job for which the person will be paid. We are allowing this person certain privileges within our home. Now suppose, after a while, this person starts to alter the contract on his own. He starts to tell us what we can eat or drink, how much electricity or water we can use, or what car we can drive. Suppose he alters the contract even more and writes a clause that permits him to take whatever property we have or that we have to pay a part of our neighbor's mortgage. Suppose he then takes control of our bank accounts and increases his salary to two to three times what our own salary is..."

"I'd have kicked him the hell out of my house as soon

UNALIENABLE

as he started telling me what to eat or drink!"

"Right, Tommy, any sane person would have done the same thing. We would not hand over our rights in our own home to a stranger. Why should we do the same at a governmental level? This is what is happening to our federal government. There are those who are using it to promote their particular interests to the detriment of the People. Do you remember a while back when we watched Charles Dickens' *David Copperfield* on TV? Do you remember that slimy character *Uriah Heep* and how he wormed his way into the household with his false humility? Our government is filled with Uriah Heeps pursuing their private interests behind the façade of government – chipping away at our liberties and eroding the original intent of the founding fathers."

He continued," Let me ask you a question. Do you think that the Constitution applies to you?"

"Well, my teacher said it was the supreme law of the land."

"It is the supreme law of the land as it applies to the federal government. The Constitution does not apply to you; it *BELONGS* to you and applies to the people within the government. You see, anyone who is employed by our government has sworn an oath to uphold it. This means that if a person makes his living from the taxpayers' money, he has effectively sworn to be a servant of the People in exchange for his salary. He has given up some of his liberties to be responsive to the People in exchange for his employment. The Constitution, whether state or federal, applies to *them*, not to *us*."

"When you were teaching, didn't you work for the government?"

"Absolutely. I worked for the county and state governments as a teacher and for the federal government when I was in the Navy. I now work for a private corporation, but when a federal grant is given to me, I am obliged to respond to the federal authority that gave me the People's money and not to my bosses at RCA."

"Did you have to swear an oath?"

"Not as a teacher, but I did sign a contract. As a *Sea Bee*, I definitely did swear an oath to uphold and defend the Constitution of the United States from all enemies, both foreign and domestic."

"When I pledge allegiance to the flag, am I swearing an oath?"

"Well, in a way you are, but in reality, you're not. The pledge is a public assertion of loyalty to the republic; the oath is a sacred and solemn promise. Although I haven't been in the Navy for a long time, I still take the oath I swore to very seriously. I've got mixed feelings with normal citizens pledging allegiance to their government; it should be the other way around. The politicians and civil servants should pledge allegiance to the People to whom they are obliged to serve. Would you pledge allegiance to the butler we were talking about? You would respect the contract, but not the personal wishes of the butler."

"Dad, you just said we didn't have a democracy. I thought that's what we had."

"No, we have a constitutional republic. Most people mistake what we have for a democracy. It was tried in the original colonies in New England and it failed miserably. Democracy has an inherent flaw; it is a system where the majority can grab complete power through democratic elections. They can vote to trample on the rights of the minority. They can impose a tyranny on everyone, including themselves. That's why our president is elected, not by a popular vote count, but by an electoral college. You may notice that practically every communist or socialist state refers to themselves as a democracy or a democratic republic. You may also notice they have only one political party. *Thomas Jefferson* called this an elected despotism. Others have called it mob rule or the tyranny of the majority."

"What we actually have is a government with limitations on its powers which are divided up among the three branches. You can tell by the amount of space dedicated to them in the Constitution their importance in the minds of the drafters. The strongest is supposed to be the legislative branch because it is the closest to the People and the States, the second is the executive and, the third and weakest is the judicial. In any case, we were supposed to have a federal government that was based upon the *rule of law*, and not the rule of a mob or of an individual."

"My teacher says that we have a two-party system - democrats and republicans. When we were talking about the butler, is this what you meant?"

"Exactly. However, the lines between what they

represent are getting blurred. There used to be a marked difference between them. Within my lifetime, the democrat party has become more socialist and the republicans are losing their conservatism."

"When I was eight, I remember President Kennedy getting assassinated. Did you vote for him?"

"Yes, I did. I also voted for Eisenhower in '52 and '56 and Barry Goldwater in '64."

"JFK was a democrat; isn't Goldwater a republican?"

"Yes."

"Which are you?"

"Neither. I'm not running for office; why would I be a member of a political party? Listen, these political parties have what is called a platform to try and convince the People that they have their best interests at heart. They represent the butler who wants me to employ him. They seek my vote to put them in office. I don't identify with my employee nor do I represent his platform to other citizens. When I vote, I vote for the person I want based upon their actions or what I believe they stand for as an individual, not their party. I voted for Ike because I knew him to be an excellent organizer and executive from the war. I voted for JFK because I believed him to be an honorable man; he was a war hero who saved the lives of the crew of his PT boat – the 109. I voted for Goldwater because of his anti-communist stance and because of that stupid atomic bomb political ad that the democrats ran. Johnson ran as a "peace" candidate and has now escalated our involvement in Vietnam, so I guess my choice was the correct one, even though he lost."

The year was 1967 and our country was entering what

could only be defined as a slow, radical turn towards open socialism. The first principles of a free society were about to be turned into nothing more than a punch line for the enlightened elitists pushing their progressive agenda. Of course, I didn't know this, nor would I have recognized it at eleven years old, but my father was more astute and observant than I. He knew where the country was going and didn't buy into the paradigm being presented by politicians, makers and shakers and pundits with Ivy League degrees. He told me that the assassination of John Kennedy was more significant than we could imagine in the breakdown of our society and could only be described as a *"coup d'etat."* Just who, today, would doubt this?

CHAPTER 8

ANARCHY

My father lived long enough to see the Berlin Wall come down. As we sat watching the events unfold on the television, he commented, "I remember when that wall went up back in 1961. Even though the war had been over for more than fifteen years and the Nazis were defeated, the communists called it 'The Anti-Fascist Wall,' as though there were any major differences between Hitler's socialism and Khrushchev's socialism. It had nothing to do with fascism. It goes to show you what lying thugs they were – they built a wall to keep people *in* and claimed its purpose was to keep other people *out*. Leave it to Marxists to name something the complete opposite of what it really is. I guarantee you that the people sealed in by that wall knew what it was for. What they never considered is that ideas are never stopped by walls. In fact, they amplify them. When I was a guard at Moyamensing, we were surrounded by walls within walls within walls and the more confined the prisoners were, the more their thoughts were concentrated on freedom. None of them deserved that freedom, but they still longed for it."

I responded, "I have a vague recollection of the wall going up too, and JFK giving that speech in Berlin but didn't know what it all meant."

He nodded, then mused, "Well, you were only five or six years old when the wall went up. It doesn't seem that long ago to me. You know, I still remember the propaganda from the war. The Russians were our valiant, heroic allies fighting the Nazis and, all of a sudden, the war ended, and they were the evil scourge trying to topple governments and enslave societies. The fact is that they were always an evil scourge, killing tens of millions of people under the guise of social justice and some impossible pipedream of a utopian ideal of equality."

My father used the remote control to turn off the television and turned his attention to me.

"I have thought about all of the conflicts and wars that I have seen in my lifetime and I have come to the conclusion that individuals rarely want to initiate wars, but once they get into government or leadership positions, they can't wait for an opportunity to spill their countrymen's blood. They'll deny this outright, but they'll propagandize their motives for starting and continuing war and they often have to convince their people that they are on the moral high ground, that either God or humanitarianism is on their side and that they are invincible."

"Looking back," he continued, "I can say without a doubt that centralized governmental authority, headed by the sociopaths and psychopaths that naturally migrate to that authority, is the greatest threat to life and liberty that human experience teaches us!"

I allowed him to continue without interruption while he detailed to me examples from history. He spoke of the histories of Greece and Rome and compared them, but he brought the idea closer to home with the history of Germany over the last couple of centuries.

"Did you know, Tommy, that before the French Invasion into Germany in 1792, there were about 250 independent states? Keep that number in mind because by the time von Bismarck unified Germany in 1871, that number had been reduced to thirty-nine, by merging and political wrangling. When the Weimar Republic was formed after the First World War, there were nineteen states represented in the Reichstag."

"To tell you the truth, I was unaware of this history," I responded. "My recollections of the history of Germany goes back to the Romans and then a brief span in the Middle Ages and then onto the 20th Century."

"Well, high school and college history classes leave a lot to be desired and are pretty scant on truth. I don't think I ever met a kid who thought it was anything more than a collection of names and dates with everything happening in a chronological order of events. History never happens that way and has no active consciousness of itself that it would order things so nicely. Mark Twain said that things never happen in the right place, at the right time and for the right reasons; historians and chroniclers correct this in hindsight! The birth, movement, and maturation of ideas and their effects are the basis of what we can learn from history. Returning to Germany, do you think a Hitler could have come to power the way he did if Germany had still been a collection of 250 independent states? He may have gotten control of one or two, but not the entire German people. It was the unification under a central government that placed all of that power within the grasp of that socialist psychopath. What was it that the Nazis declared? *'Ein Volk; Ein Reich; Ein Fuhrer!'* Authoritarians must always centrally consolidate power to force their will upon the very people they claim to want to oversee for their own good. I find it interesting that we, as a species, are more apt to crucify our messiahs and follow those who would most likely lead us to our own death and the destruction of our societies."

I did not sense any cynicism in my father's words, but rather a measured reflection upon his observations. Regardless of his understanding of human history, he was enthusiastic about humanity and our ability to eventually overcome our shortcomings and right wrongs, but he was well aware of all of our individual self-interests and moral corruption that can lead us astray. He was also well aware that the majority of societal problems were found in government controls.

"So, what do you think the answer is? I mean, if you were to set up a government, what would you suggest?" I asked.

He looked at me with a smile and answered, "Well, first, it would have to be local and second, it would be a half-step above anarchy. Our Constitution has the capability to work just fine, if adhered to honestly, but its one flaw is that it is dependent upon people of moral character occupying its positions of authority. Our founding fathers knew this quite well and tried their damnedest to provide for checks and balances and oversight to curtail immoral, human self-interests. These corrupt elected people have created agencies with regulatory authority which sidestep our legislative processes. They have nullified parts of our Constitution and are unresponsive to the People. We also have judges whose interpretations enter into law. This was never the intent of our founders. I have never met an angel, but I'm positive that none has ever been elected to a seat in government and I'm absolutely positive that none can be found in any of the government's institutions and civil services."

"At a local level," he went on, "everyone knows the individuals around them. This is why it has to be local, because your next-door neighbor's ethics can be judged on his past, personal interactions with his community. Therefore, it is less likely for him to be openly corrupt knowing that he has to live where he is elected and his actions take effect."

"I guess you're right; there isn't a more powerful deterrent than to be humiliated in front of your family and neighbors, tarred and feathered and run out of town on a rail," I responded.

He smiled, "Or worse! Another thing I might add is to never elect anyone to office who wants to be elected. I believe that there is always a sense of ulterior motives for wanting to hold an authoritative seat in the first place. As far as virtue goes, it would probably be better to select a random citizen from a hat. Maybe then we could assure, as much as possible, honesty in our representatives."

I smiled at the suggestion.

"But, what about anarchy, Dad? We wouldn't want to be without governmental order," I posited.

"Why not? What's wrong with anarchy?"

His response took me by surprise. I didn't think my father had anything good to say about anarchy.

"You know Tommy, I think anarchy has gotten a bad name but nobody ever reflects upon just what it is they object to. If you equate anarchy with social chaos, then yes, it should be avoided. If you're talking about a lack of a formal government, I believe an argument can be made to support the idea."

"When I think of anarchy, I think of the French Revolution…" I responded.

"That wasn't anarchy, Tommy, that was social chaos as a result of wrong-headed, elitist governmental abuses and the people rampaging with their pent-up frustrations once the state's defenses collapsed. There was still a provisional governmental order, but it was an irrational, populist reaction to centuries of suppression by a ruling class and the church that supported it. They merely took over the institutions of the King's government and filled them with radicals. The American Revolution was completely different in that it was a *republican* revolution – a rational response to a similar tyranny. There was no cry for "*égalité*" in the American colonies, just for freedom. We didn't want to kill the tyrant, we just wanted him to leave us alone."

"I understand that, Dad. But I know you well enough to know that you're no anarchist. All my life I've seen your rational support for the Constitution and its principles."

"You're right, I'm not an anarchist, but we are talking about a question of alternatives. If you were to ask me to choose between a socialist or a communist government and anarchy – no government at all – I'd choose anarchy every day of the week and twice on Sunday. Before I give you a couple of examples of what I mean, let me put a question to you: every once in a while, you go camping, right?"

"I used to, but haven't in a while."

"Okay, well, let's say you go camping with four of your buddies. You're all in the woods with no governmental authority around – no police, no courts, no jails, no politicians, no bureaucracies – what happens?"

"I'm not sure I know what you mean…"

"Do you and your buddies degenerate into a bunch of wild, savage animals and try to kill each other?"

"No! In fact, we are generally more cautious of one another's safety."

"So, being closer to a state of nature, or 'anarchy,' doesn't dissolve a society nor its people's sense of morality towards their group."

"Well, Dad, in that small context, I see what you mean, but what about a larger society. I mean, with five guys in the woods, if one got out of line, the other four wouldn't let him get too far…"

"Wouldn't that also be the case in a larger society?" he questioned.

"Could be. Come to think of it, I still remember you telling me when I was a kid that if I ever ran into trouble or got lost to go to the first adult I saw and ask for help. I remember when I was seven years old and I fell through the ice on a pond near a construction site and those men all stopped what they were doing to come to my aid. One of them even carried me sopping wet in his arms to our home and handed me over to Mom."

"That's my point: for every possible person there is out there with bad intentions, there are thousands of people with good will. Initially, after oppressive, government controls were pushed aside, I'm sure there would be rioting, looting, and threats to life and property. But if the honest population is armed and able to protect themselves, their property, and that of their neighbors with lethal force, these spasms would subside very quickly. They would be just as fearless in the restoration of order as the miscreants are in their destruction of everything in their path. But let me give you a couple of examples from our history. The first is of minimal government and the second is of anarchy. Have you ever read Ben Franklin's *Remarks Concerning the Savages of North America*?" he asked.

"No; I haven't."

"Well, you should. I was struck by his description of the way the indigenous Americans organized their society and by their minimalization of a formal government. Franklin became aware of the proceedings between the envoys from Virginia, Maryland, and Pennsylvania and the delegates from the Iroquois Confederacy of the Six Nations who met in Lancaster, Pennsylvania in 1744. He describes their governing structure and their procedures during their deliberations. Franklin was really taken by their respect for the opinions of others and their courtesy regarding other points of view during their council meetings. They listened without interruption to the opposing side, left without saying a word, and returned the next day to give their point of view. They left again, expecting the white men to deliberate and return the next day with their counter offer. You see, originally, the Confederation was composed of five tribal nations; their Great Law required that policies be carefully discussed. First the Senecas and Mohawks, whom they called the 'Older Brothers,' debated to reach an agreement, then the 'Younger Brothers,' the Oneida and Cayuga, debated. If the two groups disagreed, the Onondaga could cast the deciding vote. If the two groups did agree, the Onondaga would put into action the unanimous decision. If the Onondaga disagreed with the decision, they would refer the matter back to the Council. If the Council again approved their original decision, the Onondaga were overruled. Also, each nation was completely independent from the others and the confederation could not impose anything upon them without their consent and only convened in the event that they had a common problem to address. Does this all sound familiar? It was with the advice of these indigenous peoples that our system of federal government took shape."

I sat and watched my father expound on his topic, listening intently to what he had to say.

"These procedures," he went on, "were in complete contrast to the way the British carried on their parliamentary debates and Franklin found it very refreshing. It didn't end there because, in order to accept any proposal put to the councils, 75% of the men had to approve it and the final word came from the women; 75% of them also had to approve it before it would be accepted. Even John Locke was impressed by their society. He thought that it was as minimal a governmental structure as they could get while retaining their liberties and being as close to the state of nature as possible. In fact, many of the political philosophers of the day believed the same. This was not lost on our founding fathers when they drew up the Articles of Confederation and, finally, the U.S. Constitution. Sure, they had the Enlightenment as a guide, but don't underestimate the influence of the Iroquois on our form of federal government. Franklin, in particular, recognized that what the indigenous peoples lacked in technology, they more than made up for in wisdom derived from a natural existence and adherence to natural law."

"If I recall my history, there was a point in time when the Native Americans went from being 'the Noble Savages' to 'the Brutal Savages.' Just more propaganda, I guess."

"Tommy, like most groups that are being threatened, they became brutal when they were forced to. Their confederation was designed to ensure peace, not aggression, between their peoples. Did you ever ask yourself why Europeans called them 'uncivilized' and 'savages'? It was precisely because they had no formal government and all of the trappings that go along with it. I mean, they had no written laws, so there were no criminals. There were no criminals, so they didn't have a police force to arrest people, judges to judge them, or prisons to hold them. Their social order took care of any discord or injustice and it was practically instantaneous. If one of them were to commit an unacceptable act, they would be ostracized and ejected from the tribe because they were found unfit to live among the people. Would you consider this 'savagery'?"

"Dad, when we lived in Magnolia, I had some friends who were Lenni Lenape. I had many opportunities to talk with the grandfather of one of them. To tell you the truth, I never saw anything that I would call 'savage'. The *muxumsa* could talk for hours under the trees and keep us spell-bound with his stories and every one of them had a moral to teach. He never raised his voice, was very kind, and always had time for the kids."

"Well, we don't think about it anymore, but what do you think our European societies were like before the ancient republics and empires came into being? We were just as tribal as the American natives are. We, in Italy, also had bands, tribes, and nations linked by common languages, customs, and beliefs. Today, I couldn't tell you what we belong to – I never looked into it – but my father and grandfather could tell you because those traditions still resonate within those who remained in Abruzzo. Your mother's family calls themselves 'Italian,' but their part of Italy was tribally Greek..." he answered.

My father was right. In 1995, two years after his death, I went to discover what my father and his brothers never knew about their heritage. I went on this journey of discovery to fulfill a desire he had expressed to me but could not complete due to his illness and subsequent demise. With the assistance of distant relatives in Lanciano and an historian from Fossacesia, I traced our family's lineage back to the Second Crusade – some twenty-three generations. I was able to place myself into both the local and broader history of my people. To digress slightly into our family's history, I found that we, too, could identify ourselves tribally in the exact same manner in Oscan or Latin as an Oglala Sioux would in *Lakhota*. That identity lasted from before the Bronze Age all the way until the 4th or 5th century after Christ, when the Oscan language went extinct and was supplanted by Latin almost entirely. The ancestral traditions remain to this day, though the language has changed. Even language, according to my father, could be distinguished from a dialect by one feature – an army and a navy! A dominant, centralized force will always overcome a lesser one, absorbing and diluting the language of the conquered.

My father continued, "The only real problem that I can see with tribalism is that it generally leads to technological stagnation. If every neighboring tribe were to progress at an equal rate, there would be a balance of equal forces, but if one tribe develops a technology that another tribe hasn't, they'd have an advantage and would look to take control of the resources of those less capable of defending themselves. History has illustrated this clearly and repeatedly. Who knows for sure if it wasn't actually technology that led us to form governments in the first place? I mean, we did go from stone to bronze and then from bronze to iron, from iron to black powder then to the atom. As far as I know, we really began to see our societies develop armies based upon our weaponry; first for the purpose of defense and then for keeping our own populations under the control of some centralized, pyramidal hierarchy. Once this structure was solidified, we eventually went on to aggression and conquest. And, speaking of conquest, I can give you thousands of examples of how organized governments started wars and conflicts. Could you name me one anarchy that did the same? The very fact that a military organization necessarily has to be a pyramidal hierarchy already means that the fighting force is set up as a governmental structure before either defense or aggression even begins."

"Well, Dad, wouldn't you say that we need a military force to protect our people and our country?"

"Of course we do, but this doesn't always have to be the case. Militias are designed for defense; once you have a standing, professional army, aggression won't be too far behind. The tool would eventually fall into the hands of some psychopath. Now, the second example is one of anarchy: do you recall the 1849 California Gold Rush?"

"Yes, I do."

"Do you know what the circumstances were in California at the time? It was still a Mexican province after the Mexican-American War under the slack control of the U.S. Army. It wasn't a territory nor was it a state and there was no real government to speak of, just a disorganized collection of legal customs from Mexico and those introduced by American settlers. We get this picture of a bunch of wild, unruly guys, but this is only partially correct. When dealing with 'vices,' I'm sure this was the case - primarily because there were few respectable women among them to temper the men's actions. However, when dealing with possessory and property rights, it was a different story. The cry of easily found riches just waiting to be picked up caused a massive upsurge of all kinds of people from around the world. The interesting thing was that no matter how rowdy and unruly those people were, they never entered another man's tent when he was out prospecting and they never took anything from his claim, which was respected by everyone involved. It wasn't until California drafted its constitution and it was ratified into statehood that the problems of crime really began. The American prospectors passed laws to charge a fee to foreigners, such as the Chileans, the Chinese, and the French. They were forced to pay a huge twenty-dollar fee for the privilege of prospecting, whether they were successful or not. Only then did thievery become a problem. In other words, it took an act of government attempting to protect vested interests to create crime. Now, I'm not saying there was no other crime before this, but the society handled what it could and in the best way practicable. Here, I'm referring solely to property and water rights, which were considered sacred to all involved."

"You know, Dad, I've always wondered just who came up with the expression 'you can't take the law into your own hands'. It seems to me that protection is one thing, but vendetta is something else altogether."

"Think about that statement a moment: what is the difference between a self-defensive act and a vendetta?"

I thought a moment and the only thing I could come up with was *timing*.

I responded, "Well, Dad, timing!"

"That's right. Timing! You see, if someone were to react defensively the moment the aggressive act was occurring, then there would be no forethought. A vendetta is an act after the fact which requires meditation to respond against a real or perceived wrong. Let's imagine, for a moment, someone breaks into our house to burgle us and finds me alone and kills me in the process. You were not here to defend me when that act was taking place, but it riles you to no end and you go searching for the person who took your father's life. Now, let's say you identify him beyond a doubt, take a weapon, find him, and kill him. Is justice served?"

I did not hesitate in my response, "It is, to my mind."

"Does it benefit me? I'm already dead."

"Well, Dad, had I been there to defend you and kill him before he killed you, it would have. But not afterwards. The way I see it, had I gotten him before he got you, it would have benefitted you and our society at large. With you dead, only our society benefits because that person won't be able to kill another," I responded.

"That's right. Society benefits by both the defensive act at the moment of the aggression and by the vendetta. So, you have to ask yourself, 'Why would anyone believe that a vendetta is somehow a scornful act, but self-defense is not?' Is it the meditation or the fact that there was no need for police, jails, judges, lawyers, juries, and law codes? When a sheriff put together a posse of citizens to hunt down and lynch a known criminal after a murder or a horse theft, was not justice served and society protected? I think you'll find that it was not '*vigilante*' justice that 'cleaned up' the old west but stopped it from getting 'dirty' in the first place. A society in which everyone is armed and capable of defending themselves is a *polite* society. You may be able to rob a bank, but you've still got to run your horse down Main Street with a hundred armed citizens lining both sides. It may surprise you to know that there were less than a dozen bank robberies in the entire '*wild west*' from the end of the Civil War until the early 1900s. Here lies the evidence that a society is very well capable of looking after itself with only a minimal need for a government."

From these kinds of observations, my father reminded me that governments did have a role in a free society, but it should be restricted and limited only to the needs required of it. In other words, "the government that governs best, governs least!" He also reminded me that the roles of society and government have to be distinguished from one another. His examples showed me that the more a society cedes control to a government and makes itself dependent, the more crime and antisocial behavior can take root.

"But Dad," I responded, "what happens if you get it wrong and lynch the wrong guy or kill the wrong person in a vendetta? Isn't this reason to be careful with the practice?"

"Tommy, don't be naïve! The government's justice system is made up of the same fallible men as the society. If you can show me that the judicial system is much less prone to mistakes than the society that permits it to exist, I would concede your point. All systems are subject to errors and frank miscarriages of justice. When you look at all of the Supreme Court decisions and legal precedents in case law that justified things like slavery, segregation, denial of voting rights, denial of education and the like, how can anyone claim to know which is superior? I'm sure you'll find that the only difference between societal vigilantism and an organized, governmental judicial system is that, if the government makes a mistake, nobody is held accountable and the damage to society is much greater. Those responsible for injustices are hidden behind the façade of a government procedure, not the search for true justice. The real difference is that governments, by reason of sheer numbers, are actually more prone to miscarriages of justice."

He left me thinking over this observation and, once again, altered the way I viewed the 'institutions' of government, which we are all told to respect. His point was to respect the intention of the institution, but never to respect the people involved in its operation until they have earned it.

CHAPTER 9

HOW GOVERNMENT CREATES AN ENVIRONMENT FOR ORGANIZED CRIME

On Friday, the 21st of March 1980, I was in New York City having a beer with two of my friends, Jay Acovone and Jerry Le Page. It was getting late and I was about to go home when a newsflash came over the TV – Angelo Bruno was dead. The 'Docile Don' was assassinated by a shotgun blast to the back of the head as he sat in a car in front of his home at 10th Street and Snyder Avenue in South Philly.

Jay asked me if I knew the man, to which I said, "Sure, he was from my family's neighborhood in South Philly. Regardless of his 'profession,' he was well-liked and kept the neighborhood clean and safe. I think things are about to change now."

The next morning, I drove down to South Jersey to see my parents. I kept thinking about the hit driving south on the New Jersey Turnpike. My father and I had discussed '*la Cosa Nostra*' many times in the past and I didn't see how we could avoid having another discourse this weekend. Everyone knew what the situation was in South Philly; it was common knowledge that the Bruno Family had the support of the Gambino Family in New York, but that support was lost a few years earlier when Carlo Gambino died. Don Angelo had kept his family out of the drug business and had also handed over their control of Atlantic City to the New York families, knowing that his family was too weak to prevent a violent takeover. This had caused many underlings in his own family to become irate because they felt they were being left out of the action and were losing millions of dollars in income. It was only a question of time before someone made a move on Bruno. The question was whether or not it was sanctioned by the 'Commission' in New York. Whether it was or wasn't, there would be blood.

These things didn't concern me too much because we had nothing to do with the mob, but their effects would be felt from Philly to Atlantic City. I also knew that it wouldn't be long before corpses started popping up with cryptic messages as to who was involved and what role they played in the coup. This, however, would probably not be the subject of our conversation; my father was more interested in the economics of organized crime than in the morality of what they did.

It was about ten o'clock when I arrived home to find my father collating a printing job in his workshop. For some reason he never explained to me, he enjoyed printing and putting books together. He built a small printing shop attached to the house where he could escape to do his work and read in peace.

He stopped what he was doing and we went to the dining room for a cup of coffee. As we settled at the table, the conversation went directly to the events in Philly.

My father asserted, "Bruno should have known better; that business is very predictable and he had his guard down. The exact same thing happened to Julius Caesar on the Ides of March in 44 B.C. I guarantee you that it was someone very close to him that took him out. I also guarantee you that, just like Marcus Junius Brutus and Gaius Cassius Longinus, the ones that did this will also have their Battle of Philippi."

On many occasions, my father had illustrated the hypocrisy of government going after the mob using '*moral*' grounds as a motive. To him, morality had nothing to do with it; it was merely a question of revenues and protecting government turf. Interestingly, by passing legislation of which the mob could take advantage, the government's cut of the profits could not be collected legally. It took the RICO Act to give the government the hook it needed to confiscate those funds. Just where those confiscated funds wound up, nobody knows.

If one were to look at virtue and morality and apply it to government, its actions would appear schizophrenic. An example would be the sale of tobacco across state lines: the government, on one hand, makes huge revenues on tobacco sales and subsidizes its production, yet on the other hand, the government spends money to tell us tobacco is harmful to our health and bans its sale to minors. It's not the Department of Health, Education and Welfare or the Office of the Surgeon General that oversees this, but the Bureau of Alcohol, Tobacco and Firearms, a federal law enforcement organization within the United States Department of Justice. The mob puts up no pretenses and doesn't have to act hypocritically; it does what it does without claiming to be anything other than what it is.

In its purest form, organized crime is perfect entrepreneurship; it sees a demand in society and satisfies it. In fact, it wouldn't be called 'organized crime' if it weren't for the fact that a law had to be passed giving them a potentially profitable reason to set up a business in the first place. In practically every enterprise that satisfies the demands of vice-based activities, such as drugs, prostitution, numbers writing, gambling, or alcohol during the Prohibition, the business opportunities of organized crime are closely linked to government legislation which interferes with the natural liberties of the People. Also, the mob cannot make an income from these vices if people don't voluntarily hand over their money for the services and products it provides. This is in direct contrast with the government, which forces everyone to lighten their pockets with the threat of fines, the seizure of property, or the threat of imprisonment for disobeying its edicts.

My father would often ask me which we are to consider 'immoral' in these cases, the invasive law or the activities countering that law? Which are we to consider more harmful and destructive to society?

It is only when the mob becomes involved in extortion, loan sharking, murder for hire, and racketeering that they can be considered immoral because they are using force or the threat of violence to take what doesn't belong to them. In this sense, however, the 'mob' is no more immoral than any government doing the same through the ratification of laws which violate the spirit and letter of constitutional restraints.

Additionally, so called 'black markets,' in which goods or services are traded illegally, cannot exist without government meddling in the market. The most obvious cause for operating in covert economies is to trade contraband or to sidestep price controls and rationing. This is the direct result of government interference. In most cases, owning the product, or availing oneself of the service, is, in itself, not illegal, but either the production or the means of getting those products or services is impeded or banned by government dictate. This was the case with alcohol during Prohibition and gasoline during World War II or the 'Corn Laws' in 19th century England, for example.

In cases where the government fixes prices for goods and services below the true, competitive market value, legitimate producers will either stop their production, reallocate their resources to produce other goods uncontrolled by the government's edict, lay off their workers, or even close their shops because they would lose money continuing their pre-regulation activities. This would eventually result in a scarcity of their products in the legal market.

A typical scenario would be that the government, because of some special interest pressure or because of some socialistic ideology, would order a fixed price of some necessity, rendering it unresponsive to market pressures. This action is cheered on by those in society who want "something for nothing". That 'something' then starts to appear less and less on the supermarket shelves. The "scarcity" then prompts those with the means to create the underground market to provide the goods, usually at prices that are far higher than they would have been had the government not intervened. The "shortages" would then create an outcry in society, forcing those in government to respond. The politicians in government would then construct a campaign in the media to blame the "evil" entrepreneurs, capitalists, or the "free" market as the culprit. Their solution is always that the government has to take control of the *means* of production, obviously to be regulated through some new bureaucracy. It is from this point that the real damage to the taxpayer and the domestic consumer begins.

The government will either create new, or confiscate the existing, means of production and hire a tax-funded management and workforce to produce the promised good. Usually, to organize the production, the upper and middle management will be populated by incompetent bureaucrats in short-sleeved shirts and clip-on neckties wielding clipboards with no practical experience in business or industry. The workforce, being unionized, government employees, will be paid wages much higher than their private sector counterparts. The end result is that the goods or service in question will be subject to inefficient allocation of resources, higher production costs, and reduced quality from a de facto, non-competitive, government monopolization. This monopoly, without a free market to indicate demand and with no regard for profitability, will only concern itself with the production of quantity, as it is the only measure

UNALIENABLE

available to them. The taxpayers will bear the cost of it all, sometimes at least five times the original, free market costs.

In the end, what was originally one dollar per unit in the free market and was promised at fifty cents, will now cost every taxpayer five dollars to produce, regardless of whether the consumer wanted to purchase the product or not. The shelf price of fifty cents, then, is merely an illusion; it is what the consumer perceives the price to be. He is actually paying $5.50 rather than the original one dollar if he purchases and $5.00 if he doesn't.

It is, however, a great deal for those who are not taxpayers or for those in foreign countries looking to import the goods to their internal markets; their purchases are subsidized to create a price below the free market value at the expense of our domestic taxpayer, creating an unnatural drain on our own domestic resources.

Imagine going into a candy store with a five-year-old and asking if he would like to purchase that one-dollar candy bar for fifty cents. He would obviously say 'yes' to the proposition. Then imagine telling him that he'd have to pay $5.00 in order to pay that fifty cents. It is unlikely that even a child would see the logic of paying $5.50 for a candy bar that he could have purchased for a dollar. Not even the mob could be this diabolical.

My father had always made his views on the mafia very clear. There were two concepts he wanted me to understand whenever the subject arose.

The first was that, when dealing with vices, the mafia and the government always operate in symbiosis with one another. Those in government will perpetuate the invasive laws that they know are damaging to society as a whole and are in violation of natural liberties just to keep their bureaucracies operating. Meanwhile, the mafia will continue providing the goods and services as long as there is a willing market demand. The mafia will cheer on even more invasive laws because it provides more profitable business opportunities. Additionally, the more effective the government becomes at enforcement, the higher the profits will be for the mob because they can claim that external pressures reduced the supply, raising the prices of the products in demand. They then earn more for less. It works 'hand in glove'.

The second was that, when dealing with true, criminal violations of our liberties, those in government and those in the mafia exhibit only a difference in scale; the government is much more damaging to society than the mafia. They both occupy the same echelon of immorality, but government has a total monopoly on hypocrisy. It commits with impunity what society would consider criminal if done by the mob or by individuals and what the government itself would codify into law as criminal. Additionally, the movers and shakers in government are immune from prosecution.

My father once gave me an example of this notion. He told me that if he and I were walking down the street, entered a grocery store, and ordered the owner to pay us 45% of his gross earnings yearly or we'd bust him and his store up, we'd be committing an obvious criminal act. When the government does it, however, they're just looking for the owner's 'fair share' of taxes. The question that is never asked is this: just who in government determines what that 'fair share' is?

UNALIENABLE

It was my father's opinion that no such thing exists; when one is being robbed, it is usually the thief that is in the position to determine the amount. Additionally, the thief only robs you once; the government robs you every day.

CHAPTER 10

It Was Just Applied Wrong

In 1969, I was in the 8th grade. It was a time when the world seemed to be in a constant muddle. The television news was confusing to me and I couldn't follow anything without having to ask my father the meaning of what I was hearing and watching. All of the kids I knew had some superficial interpretation of the events of the day, parroting whatever the older teens and rock stars had to say about the world.

To me, no matter how seriously they thought their cerebral attempts were to justify a growing disdain for the country, they were just unwitting pawns furthering some hidden agenda. I was too young to identify that agenda, but I was sure that a kid, who two years before had been playing little league and pinning baseball cards to grate against the spokes of his bike tires, could not possibly have a well-reasoned, intellectual opinion on world events. For me, it was even more perplexing because of my understanding of what the world had gone through in the years before my birth in 1955.

I was raised surrounded by neighbors and men in my own family who had served in all of the branches of the armed forces during the Second World War. They were strong-willed and hardened. There was nothing frivolous about them. All of them knew why they fought and had no apologies to offer.

Some of our neighbors were even refugees who had seen first-hand, as civilians, the horrors of that war.

As an example, the family that lived across the street from us in Magnolia were Dutch immigrants from a small town outside of Rotterdam. Henk and Ena Groot were in their early teens when the Nazi army took control of their homeland with the assistance of like-minded socialists in their own country. Henk told us of the hardships, privations, and atrocities committed against his people by the German National Socialist *Wehrmacht*. His way out was to join the U.S. Army at war's end as a foreign national and seek U.S. citizenship once he was assigned to Fort Dix. The Groots were strict Orthodox Presbyterians and held unshakably solid Christian values, but Henk's Christian convictions were just not strong enough to forgive the Germans that occupied his country. He knew evil when he saw it and wanted nothing more to do with Europe or socialism. America, for him and his family, represented salvation and freedom.

One evening, while watching the news, I described to my father what was happening around me and how I felt that something was wrong with the way the kids were talking about things they couldn't possibly know about. I also told him that the kids were expressing a growing disgust and, at times, an outright hatred for our country. Even some of the teachers were implying that the country was somehow immoral for its opposition to communism and socialistic opinions of "justice". This view was in stark contrast to my own, which I held in my mind for good reasons. I could not understand how they, having been raised in the same environment as I had been, could come to a completely opposite view of America.

As my father explained, "What you're seeing is the steady infiltration of Marxist propaganda spreading slowly through society, which is becoming more open. It is a creeping subversion of our principles and our trust in our government. Of course, they won't dare call it that, but don't be confused by the names they give to it. Marxism wears many different masks, but they all have the same face underneath. The reason it is known by so many different names is that once it fails in one place, another name has to be given to it to keep the agenda going."

"Dad, I'm not sure I follow what you're saying. What names are you talking about?"

"Well, Marx called it '*communism*,' the Russians called it '*Bolshevism*,' then '*Leninism*' and then '*Stalinism*' and then simply '*socialism*.' In China, it's called '*Maoism*.' The Germans called it '*Nazism*' and the Italians, '*Fascism*.' In England, it's '*Fabian socialism*.'

Here in the U.S., it's called '*progressivism*' or '*liberalism*,' like they have anything to do with classical liberal thought. The reason they use these deceitful names here is because they want to deflect from the fact that they openly supported the crimes and bloodshed of the revolutions and wars in other parts of the world that their ideology caused. I remember clearly how Mussolini and Hitler were the golden boys of the Democrats during the New Deal and how their pictures appeared on the covers of magazines before the war. Did you know that Hitler was *Time* magazine's '*Man of the Year*' in 1938?"

"Doesn't everybody know about Hitler and Mussolini and what they did to the world? How can anybody side with them?"

"…Well, what about Stalin, Tommy? He was arguably worse than either Hitler or Mussolini and he was our ally. The mistake that most people make is associating the atrocities with the name of the leader and not with their political ideas. It becomes easy to then say, 'It was their fault; they just applied it wrong.' Those convinced or brainwashed about socialism will never admit that their utopian ideas are founded in deception, theft, and violence and that these people applied it precisely as it was designed to be applied. It is a sick joke to think that the results will be different if only the name of the leader changes. Only the mentally ill would expect a different outcome by repeating the same mistakes over and over again."

Over the course of many further conversations, my father's discussions on socialism became more and more profound while my ability to understand the concepts enhanced as I grew older and became more aware of the players involved in the debate.

My father was not one to take the word of someone else in forming opinions and had the literature of those he opposed, as well as those he agreed with, in his library.

He evaluated Marx from two different perspectives: there was Marx the organizer of society and then there was Marx the economist. His observation was that there was nothing original or ground-breaking to be found in his approach to organizing society and that Marx was inspired to create his 'class struggle' construct on Georg Hegel's political theories. My father described Hegel as nothing more than a brown-nosing, court jester stuffing his face at the dinner table of the Prussian Crown.

"There are those who will tell you that Marx's concepts on organizing society go all the way back to Plato's *Republic*; don't be fooled. There is nothing approaching the nobility of ancient, Greek thought in Marx," he once told me, "and even Plato based his political views on an ignoble, ideal society where 90% of the population was slaves and chattel."

When I asked what Hegel contributed to Marx's views on a socio-political level, my father boiled it all down to the role of the individual, his family, and the origin of rights.

"Hegel," he told me, "was of the opinion that the state was the origin of our rights and that freedom could only be found in the perfection of the state through a process of struggle. In other words, you come up with an argument, pit it against a counterargument, and arrive at a conclusion – what is referred to as a Hegelian Dialectic. You then take that conclusion and pit it against another counterargument and so on and so on. The process is a continual struggle towards the perfection of the state. You may notice that the process never ends and the state can never be perfected. To me, it has always sounded like the machinations of an insane mind."

When I told him that this concept was not new to me and that the ancient Greeks also posed the dialectic of thesis, antithesis, synthesis, he responded that that was where Hegel got it. Whereas the Greeks used it to arrive at truth, Hegel applied it as a way to justify a monarch's sovereignty and control over his people through a logical process which begins with the presumption that the state is superior to the individual. By trying to ingratiate himself to some Prussian prince and other European monarchs, this false premise of the ruler being a superior human to everyone else renders his whole philosophy a farce.

He went on, "If you were to read the motto of the Fascists in Italy – '*Tutto nello stato, niente al di fuori dello stato, nulla contro lo stato*' – you'd get an idea of what Hegel's views were. This translates to 'Everything within the state, nothing outside of the state, nothing against the state.' Hegel proposed that all of human aspirations, needs, and desires must be aligned within the goals of the state. Collective will, guided by some higher and unquestionable authority, was to trump any individual will for the good of society. Under this idea, the state could only continue by replacing individual identity with a group identity in competition against another group for positive rights. Marx fixed that conflict as a class struggle between what he defined as the workers of the world, or proletariat, and the middle-class, or bourgeoisie."

I had heard these terms before, but I needed further clarification.

"In the mind of Marx, these were the two classes that he believed would enter into an economic conflict. Keep in mind that he conveniently left out the ruling class and nobility from his equation, just as Hegel did before him. Also, remember that he was using Europe as a model and that we here in America had already freed ourselves from this structure. He defined the proletariat as those only able to contribute their labor and offspring to society. They owned nothing and were supposedly not free to move from the caste they were born into. The bourgeoisie were the land, property and business owners, the shopkeepers and professionals that lived in the towns and cities. Marx never mentions that this class of people had probably come from the same proletariat that he claimed was incapable of improving their lives on their own. They were the driving force behind free market enterprise interested in protecting their positions and improving the futures of their children. Marx had promised his followers that there would be an overthrow by the exploited class of workers by the end of the 1900s, creating an outcry by the masses for the government to take over the means of production. This never came because his construct was a completely false notion. By the time the First World War had come and gone, his followers had to do something about this dilemma; it seemed that the so-called exploited workers didn't cooperate or didn't see themselves as exploited and had no desire to overthrow anything or anyone."

When I asked why Marx claimed the working people were exploited if they didn't feel they were, my father replied with a knowing smile.

"It was because Marx did what every other socialist who came after him does. He kept the word and changed the definition. His characterization of exploitation was a false economic notion and not an actual one. His definition of exploitation is not the one that immediately comes to mind to a normal person."

"How did he define it then?"

"To Marx, exploitation of the worker was defined as 'any amount of money earned by the business or factory owner above and beyond what the worker was paid to produce the product or service.' Is the idea clear to you?"

"You mean, *profits*? Why would anyone start a business if not to make a profit?"

"No one would! People start businesses to improve their lives and those of their families and not to provide jobs for other people. The idea, however, is a bit more complicated than that. If you look at the actual, real world situation, when a worker does his job, he gets paid on a timely basis for what he does; the owner has to wait to get paid after the product goes to market and is sold.

UNALIENABLE

He may not even get the retail value he was hoping for because he is in competition with others producing the same product. Also, the worker takes no financial risks in the purchasing of primary materials, the payment of rents, taxes, bank loans, utilities, tools, and machinery for the general operations of the company. Now, what would you say if I told you that any attempt by the owners to improve their company's productivity by private capital investment would be detrimental, in the mind of Marx?"

My father smiled and raised his eyebrows waiting for an answer from me. I smiled back and indicated for him to continue.

"Okay, now let's imagine that a worker is able to make one pair of shoes in an hour and he is paid two dollars per hour. Now, let's imagine that that pair of shoes has a market value of five dollars. Marx would claim that the exploitation of the worker would be the three-dollar difference. By making a capital investment in a machine that can be operated by the same worker to produce five pairs of shoes in one hour, with him still being paid that two dollars, the owner would take in twenty-five dollars. To Marx, the exploitation of the worker is then increased to twenty-three dollars! Can you see why he claimed that capitalism increases the exploitation of the working man? What he ignores is that the market price of the shoes will come down as the supply goes up and the market demand remains the same. It will come down even more once the demand drops because the number of pairs of shoes sold saturates the market still further.

Even the man making the shoes can easily afford to buy a pair. Do you understand the concept?"

"I think I do."

"You see, the rule of thumb in business is that any worker must earn for your company at least five times what you are paying him to justify his employment. This means that he is now worth five dollars an hour to operate the machine, expending much less physical labor than before. So, if the man is paid two dollars an hour and wants to buy a pair of shoes at five dollars, he must work two and a half hours. If his salary is then justifiably increased to five dollars per hour, and the price of shoes eventually drops to two-fifty, he only has to work thirty minutes for that same pair of shoes. These actions invalidate Marx's idea that labor determines the value of what is made. Although Marx was deluded, he wasn't stupid; he realized that you couldn't equivocate product for product, as far as their usefulness as a commodity goes, so the only thing he was left to render equal was a laborer's active production time. Everything falls apart trying to do this, because some workers' time is more valuable to industry and to society than others when producing what society wants or needs. The value that people place on things is subjective and can never be forced to have equal value merely because of the time and labor required to produce them. The shoes that took an hour to make have more value to society than the loaf of bread that requires the same hour to produce. Marx's entire premise is based upon this false labor theory of value. So, in the end, the working men couldn't really say they were being exploited, in the traditional sense of the word. They saw their lives as improving! Marx's followers couldn't convince them otherwise, so another strategy was needed to convince the average man to accept their government controls on the economy in order to organize their society through political means. It took Mussolini, and then Hitler, to change the paradigm from a class struggle to a national struggle."

"From its onset, Marxism could never make sense in our country," my Dad continued, "Firstly, because here in America, there were no classes; there was no royalty or nobility, no Dukes, Earls, Barons, and so on. With the exception of the Democrat-run slave states, everyone was free to follow his desires to achieve whatever he wanted in life. Marx's fundamental construct had even less meaning here than it did in Europe. Secondly, we have a constitution that reflects our conviction that the smallest minority is the *individual,* and not a select group. Our Natural Rights are God-given, negative rights, meaning that in order for me to express them, all other people have to do is refrain from stopping me! You see, our rights are considered unalienable, whereas Marx considered all rights as merely privileges granted by a governmental authority. Our system was designed to serve the citizen, not rule over us, which is why it will never be compatible with socialism, by whatever name they want to call it. Our founders would not have conceived of a government as the source of rights to grant to the citizenry, having just thrown one tyranny off; the government was to have only the privileges that we, the People, grant to it to act upon on our behalf. This is why our founders created a new form of government to fit with our aims, rather than trying to modify the pre-existing institutions of the king's government and simply replace the people running them. Can you now understand why the socialist has to get rid of God as the source of our rights, why Marx called religion 'the opiate of the people?' If a state were actually the source of our rights, we would need permission to express them; those are, by definition, not rights, but privileges or *entitlements*. These positive rights require that someone else has to be involved, firstly by dividing services or resources for distribution and permitting me to use it, secondly by forcefully denying it to someone else, and thirdly by reserving the authority to take it away from me at any time for whatever reason. Always remember, positive rights necessarily require a government; negative rights only require a society which agrees to leave each member alone."

There were many times, while I was an impressionable student, that my schooling had me convinced that what I believed to be rights weren't actually what my educators told me they were. My father was highly knowledgeable about education and I once blurted out that I had a right to it. When my father looked at me and raised his eyebrows, I knew another lesson was coming.

"So, you think you have a right to an education? Can you name me the person that God assigned to you to teach you from your birth? Can you even show me where that supposed right is in the federal or state's constitution? You do not have a right to an education, Tommy; you may not be *denied* an education, should you want one. There is a difference. By saying you have a right to one means that someone else has to either pay for it or provide it to you. If you want a formal education, there is no reason in the world that you shouldn't pay for it yourself by any means necessary. What happens when people believe they have such a right? Firstly, committees of people with institutional and personal agendas are formed to determine just what it is you are to study – they control the material. Then, anyone can enter into the programs they wish to enter, regardless of merit. When the resources are limited, others who are qualified will be denied seats in favor of preferred groups who are less qualified. At the end of the prescribed course of study, diplomas will be issued to people who don't actually deserve them. Incompetence and mediocrity will become the rule and the diploma will become less and less a valuable measure of ability."

"What if you can't find or earn the money to pay for it?"

"That's unlikely, Tommy. You can always find a way to finance a formal education that you are ultimately responsible for without taking something away from someone else. That is, assuming the diploma is more important to you than the knowledge you are seeking in a given subject. There is nothing standing in your way to study something on your own for your own personal improvement. I've done it many times. All you have to do is pick up a book and start reading. That's the reason we have public libraries."

The logic of his argument on education was watertight. I could see it being applied to many ideas. The subtle, leftist propaganda had led me to believe that entitlements were actually rights.

On the subject of propaganda, my father made it clear that socialist states rely heavily on a constant flow of one-sided half-truths and omissions surrounding big lies to convince people of their "love for humanity" and "justice" of their cause. The simple question no one answers is, "How, then, does their sense of 'justice' and 'love for humanity' lead them to commit hundreds of millions of murders in violent revolutions, wars, and social purges?"

The clear flaw of this obviously glaring truth in the face of their propagandistic lies is that when people of common sense hear them, they can't turn a deaf ear to the dishonesty. If these people cannot be persuaded by attempts at indoctrination using simple falsehoods, they must be re-educated by more forceful means: they are denied work, walled off in ghettoes, and arrested to be sent to work camps, gulags, and jails as political prisoners. If they don't bow down under this pressure, they are simply killed, adding their souls to those already eliminated by the ones in control. Is it any wonder that Lenin said their objectives necessarily required "oceans of blood" in order to be accomplished? Fear, then, becomes the glue holding the mass of society in control by a relatively small minority of wise overlords in government.

UNALIENABLE

"Self-evident truths," he told me, "don't need propaganda. You don't need to convince people that being free to follow their own desires without interference from a government is better than being oppressed."

My father had often detailed the differences between the roles of government and society and why those of society should not be handed over to government if a people were to remain free. I did have to ask him, though, if socialism *could* be applied without all of the terror historically associated with it. He told me that, on paper, it may work, but only if certain conditions are met and people are willing to compromise their freedoms and securities. Also, to start with, you'd have to completely detach economics from politics.

"The first condition that should be applied is non-coercion; people should have the ability to express their natural rights unimpeded and without prejudice or punishment. If they don't agree with government controlling everything in their lives, their freedom to leave their country at will should be guaranteed. We saw this work out effectively in Northern Italy during the '*Rinascimento*.' Allowing people the freedom to 'vote with their feet' resulted in one of the greatest blossoming of the sciences, arts, and culture the world has ever seen."

He continued, "The second condition is that the society should be as homogenous as possible; the people have to agree upon certain values as universal. These must be accepted, voluntarily, by all, otherwise discord will always be fomenting under the surface. The first condition should be the relief valve for the second."

"Dad, you mean like what the Germans tried to do?"

"No, no, no, I don't mean that. What I mean is that the people, regardless of their racial, religious, or historical cultural differences, should have a common bond of some kind that won't conflict with their free expressions of their natural rights. We have *the Right to Life, Liberty and the Pursuit of Happiness* as our common bond, for example. Everyone can agree to these principles. If people want to use these to justify government-run social programs as a form of enlightened self-interest that would be enough."

The most important condition he expressed was in terms of economic controls. This, in his view, was the major chink in the armor of socialist dogma.

He explained, "Looking at the lessons of history, there are three ways to set up a government with control over entitlements and its relationship to the economy: total economic control, partial economic control, and no economic control. The communist model of economics places capitalism, or the investment of monies into the means of production, solely into the hands of ministries or committees. This centralization is doomed to failure because they are investing other people's money without regard to its value. Furthermore, it is wasteful, subject to corruption, and to irresponsible allocation. Finally, the lack of a profit motive leaves no way to measure success beyond the quantity of what is produced. They always talk about centralized five-year plans and how many tractors they'll produce, for example, whether they're needed or not. They applaud wildly at the plan, but there is no fanfare at the end of the five years when they realize that they have fallen short of their goals. The quantity eventually becomes so important that they care little if the tractors even run or break down with their first use, as long as the numbers are met."

He continued, "What the Fascists and Nazis have shown us is that, by leaving the means of production principally in private hands but under rigid government oversight and coercion, social entitlements worked a little bit better, but were still unsustainable and still subject to corruption. In other words, the merging of corporate and government interests, which is how Mussolini himself defined Fascism, still placed the government in a dictatorial role where the autocrats determined what and how much was to be made and at what price it was to be sold. Businesses were under a continual threat of seizure and nationalization if they did not comply, and were inhibited by large, government bureaucracies. Industries that had a national importance had priorities for resources and were heavily subsidized and competition was made more difficult. Eventually, however, the financial support for their social entitlements follow those of the communists: larger and larger percentages of the population are employed in the administration of the bureaucracies and the tax revenues go towards paying government employees who produce mountains of paper and red tape, but no wealth. Also, when their internal resources wane, they'll look to the conquest of their neighbors as a source of forced labor and theft of their resources to reduce costs. If the Germans didn't have access to slave labor and the spoils from those they conquered during the war, their system would have collapsed much more quickly than it did."

My father explained to me that the closest approach to providing all of the entitlements promised by the socialists was for there to be a completely free market and a private capitalist economy with no governmental interference. He added to this that the government should have no control over the production of money or credit and that there should be no centralized banking system. These conditions are partially met in what he called the "Scandinavian Model."

"Many people would look at the Scandinavian countries and claim they are an example of the success of socialism. They are not. Those countries have relatively free markets and there is no centralized governmental control over the means of production. They are merely examples of top-heavy governments with massive, expensive social entitlement programs supported by extremely high tax rates. If the people don't mind handing over 80 to 90% of their income to the government agencies for them to provide entitlements in return, things may work out. Those in government happily justify this by saying, 'we're only paying for things you would have paid for anyway.' Of course, this is a falsehood because personal choice is ignored and because what people pay into the system, say for a retirement pension or for a health service, is being paid out for others in society who have already retired or are under medical care. Someone else will pay in the future for those working today who will retire or become ill tomorrow. However, this necessarily requires a stable number in the population or an increase in population growth, otherwise the system will fail. Even so, eventually the people will understand that they are more capable of handling their own money and spending it where they wish more efficiently than a nameless bureaucrat."

There were two more insurmountable flaws in dealing with government-provided entitlements, regardless of whether they were voluntarily accepted by the citizenry or not: *what tax rate is fair and, in the end, human nature.*

My father then touched on the subject of financing the government-controlled entitlement programs.

"Unless those in government are held constantly under public scrutiny, an unbridled ability to increase taxes will always be their easiest solution for every problem. They never think in terms of reducing expenses because there seems to be an unending flow of money from those taxed. If they want to hide their tax increases, and they have borrowing authority from a central bank, they surely will borrow. The bank then issues paper money and credit which robs everyone through inflation and interest paid on the loans. Here in the U.S., we have progressive taxation, meaning the more you earn, the greater the percentage of those earnings you pay. This is inherently unfair because it punishes the producers in society and rewards those who don't produce! It also takes away any incentives for non and low producers to work to achieve more for themselves and frustrates the producers. They will look for a break-even point of production following the Law of Diminishing Returns. The producers will then only produce as much as necessary to minimize their burden rather than as much as possible to increase their wealth and society, as a whole, will suffer."

When I asked about the possibility of a flat tax being a fairer method, he responded, shaking his head.

"A flat tax, where everyone pays a fixed percentage, is just as unfair. Firstly, who sets the percentage – is it 10, 20, 70%? If it is a high rate, the lower income earners will have nothing left to spend on their necessities of life. If it is a low rate, the wealthier and higher income earners will pay an unevenly higher amount for the same services as those who pay much less or not at all. As an example, let's say there is a service that not everyone uses over the course of any given year, like health care. Now let's say that I earn $20,000 per year and you earn $100,000. At a 10% flat tax, I would be paying $2,000 and you would be paying $10,000. Now, did you know that private insurance companies, on average, pay out only about 15% in claims on what they earn in premiums in a year? There is a high probability that, if we were both younger than thirty, neither of us would need medical services and both of us would lose out because that yearly expense is not rolled over into the next year if we don't use it. This harms me more than you, my income being less than yours, because I could have used that money elsewhere for other things. But let's say we both need the same medical service in a given year and that service, in a free market, would have cost us $500 out of pocket. Both of us are harmed, but to differing degrees, I by $1,500 and you by $9,500. Now, multiply that yearly expense over your working life. Do you see the dilemma? Whether you are willing to be stolen from or not, theft will always be theft. The proponents of these types of services will keep insisting they are free, but they are only free to those who never pay in and only of true benefit to those who suffer catastrophic health care needs. Even this would cost less, over time, with competing insurance companies in a free market."

I then asked him if there was a fair way to pay for these social services. His answer came as little surprise to me.

"Frankly, no. There is no fair way to pay for them, only a relatively equitable way. The only way that I can see to do this is to have the government enumerate all of the entitlements, total up their individual expenses, and divide that sum by the total number of people in society. The government must produce a precise, yearly budget based on that number. Add to this the expenses of the basic functions of government – maintaining an army and a navy, the courts and police services, and so on. Since a government is technically a non-profit organization, any remaining monies at the end of the fiscal year should then be rolled over into the following year and subtracted from that year's operating expenses to reduce the cost to the taxpayer. Heads of households must accept responsibility for every member of their immediate family for these per capita expenses. This is the only equitable way to apply these programs, but I know that even this would lead to predictable negative effects upon society, primarily upon families and population growth."

I could understand what my father was referring to by the predictable consequences these programs would have under this form of financing. It was then that I posed an observation and a question to him.

"You know Dad, the socialists seem good at recognizing problems in society and bringing them into public view. I mean, people who are well off don't usually think about things like unemployment, homelessness, malnutrition and the like. Don't you think the programs they propose are, at least, based in good intentions? What would you do to combat these things, if it were up to you?"

"Well," he started, "it *is* up to me! What makes you think the well-off don't have those things constantly on their minds? I fought ignorance by making sure I got an education. I used that education to combat unemployment by making sure I have a job. I fight homelessness by making sure that I have a home, hunger by having food on my table. You see, the underlying basis of being free is to be responsible for the choices that I, as an individual, make. It is not up to me, or to my government, to make choices for others or to be responsible for the consequences of the bad choices that others make. It is not up to my government to become a surrogate parent and provide a carefree existence for people as though they were irresponsible children. Now, you've just said that the socialists are good at recognizing problems in society that have to be addressed; I would counter that by saying they are good at *emotionally exploiting* problems in society that have always been recognized and have rarely been ignored. The underlying motive has nothing to do with their good intentions for people: it is merely used as a thesis for that Hegelian dialectic we spoke about. The only actual question is whether a free market, societal solution is better than their socialistic, governmental solution. History has shown us that no other system, presently known, can improve the living conditions of the common man better than a free market, capitalistic one. We, in this country, had no federal taxation from our founding until 1913, with the exception of a tax act from 1861 until 1872, which was found to be unconstitutional and eliminated. Yet, at the same time, during the 19th and early part of the 20th centuries, our country had a great explosion of charitable and philanthropic institutions, a huge number of private universities and colleges were founded and innumerable hospitals and clinics, museums and libraries came into being. Organizations like the Red Cross, the Salvation Army, the Boy Scouts, 4H, and countless others were created. In fact, you would be hard pressed to find any well-established institution in this country that was not born during this time frame. I would remind you that not a single penny from public tax monies went into these things. How? The answer is very simple: individuals in society recognized a problem to be addressed, like-minded individuals with the same values identified the cause, organized themselves, raised the funds, and set in motion their private, institutional responses. As an example, religious and charitable organizations created hospitals, along with private medical, homeopathic, osteopathic and chiropractic college faculties. Their services were either free of charge or funded by patient donation, but they operated primarily by the private funding of generous members of society. All government had to do was get out of their way. I can easily show you that the private sector is much better at dealing with the problems in society than a government is. Also, they are much more efficient, better run, and completely voluntary."

His discussion then turned to the human psyche and the effects that socialism has upon the productive people of a society.

"I think that the most damaging aspect of socialism is its effects upon the human spirit," he sighed, "If you were to go to any zoo and look at any caged, majestic animal, you'd see how pathetic and depressed they are. The same thing happens with us. If you take away a person's ability to choose and order them to take what you give them, you wind up breaking their spirit and taking away their human dignity. It is human nature to know when we are being stolen from and being ordered around against our will. Look at the bleak environment that those on the other side of the Iron Curtain are forced to live in. Look at how they are required to abide by laws and edicts of their polit bureaus without recourse. They are in a cage and the only real freedom they have is to get drunk or kill themselves. Even in the Scandinavian countries, where they are unquestionably freer than in the Soviet Union and are not actually under a socialistic economy, they still have the highest rate of suicide and alcoholism in Western Europe. This, in itself, is something to reflect upon because if this is the result of Utopia, I think most people would run from it."

My Dad gave me the clearest and simplest definition of Marxism, and all of its permutations, in this way: It is a system of economics and government for bums designed by a bum! Since then, every time I hear people screaming for "their rights" at the expense of others, this phrase immediately pops into my mind.

CHAPTER 11

THE SOCIALIST IN THE CLASSROOM

In September 1970, I entered Cherry Hill High School West as a freshman. There seemed to be an equal mix of male and female teachers on the school's faculty. Many of the men were veterans from the Second World War, the Korean War, and the Vietnam conflict. The math, science, gym, and shop teachers never really got into social issues or politics. It was a completely different case with the English and Social Studies faculties, however. My father had prepared me well as to what awaited me with these "Liberal Arts types," as he called them.

In the beginning, high school was a frightening place. Suddenly, I found myself on the lowest rung of a school hierarchy where some of the upperclassmen looked more like adults than students. Between periods, the hallways were jammed with students going to and from their lockers and then to their next classes. Being small in stature, I tried to keep as low a profile as possible. The friends that I had in junior high school were scattered throughout and I could only really associate with them at lunch or at recreation. Study hall was held in the school's auditorium. There were no desks to write on and very little studying was done. It was more like forty-five minutes of punishment for an infraction no one had committed. For some reason, no one was permitted to speak. In any case, for me, being silent had its advantages. That all changed one Friday, however, in my freshman social studies class. I found myself having to apply what my father taught me about his approach to critical analysis.

About mid-year, we were given an assignment to read *The Jungle* by Upton Sinclair. Sinclair had died two years before and our teacher was very enthusiastic about the message of this book, though it was published back in 1906. The book tells the story of a family of Lithuanian immigrants in Chicago whose pursuit of the American Dream is shattered by wage slavery, illness, injustice, misery, and untimely death. It is all tied together with an underlying hatred of capitalism, which is depicted as the fundamental cause of all the ills of society as exemplified by the meat-packing district of the city – at least this is what our teacher tried to show using this book as proof.

With the discussion that followed, the teacher asked the class what we each had thought of the book and its message. Invariably, they all found it to be a telling indictment of the evils of capitalism, which was never defined, and of the injustices perpetrated by the greedy owners of businesses to the detriment of the workers. The teacher, who was a relatively young man in his early thirties, seemed satisfied with their responses as though he had accomplished a mission. He then wanted the opinions of someone who rarely participated in classroom discussions and called upon me. My views were not what he expected.

"Mister Giordano, do you have any opinions on this book?"

"Well, it made me laugh."

"It made you laugh?"

"Yes, it did. I read it for what it was - a comedy. Granted, it was a black comedy, but a comedy nonetheless."

"How can you call this book a comedy? A lot of smart people over the last sixty years have taken this book pretty seriously. It has even led to changes in the laws for consumer protection in food production."

"I can't help that. If those smart people in government want to base laws on fantasies and the imaginings of novel writers, and if the People have no objections, that's *their* business."

"I don't think you understand the messages that Sinclair was trying to send to the public. This was a book that illustrated the unfairness of the system and the greed of the rich under laissez faire capitalism," replied my teacher.

"No, no, I understood perfectly what he was trying to say. I'm saying that it was a total fantasy. It was a pack of lies that falls flat on its face when you look at it clearly. Would you like a few examples of what I mean?"

He responded in an elitist tone, "Please do. Enlighten us all."

"Okay, let's begin at the beginning. Let's talk about Rudkus. He came to this country from Lithuania. Why?"

"He was looking for the promise of a better life here."

"I would ask you then, 'Who promised him a better life?' There is no 'promise' of a better life. There is only a better environment for opportunities. But, let's just say that Lithuania sucked and he wanted to leave. He voted with his feet to see if he could improve his conditions, buy a home, and raise a family. He made a choice and following that choice, he ended up in Chicago. Why Chicago? I mean, of all the places he could have gone, why did he go there?"

"Probably for family reasons."

"Okay, so, whatever the reason, he goes to Chicago. Again, it was his personal choice. So, then he decides to get married to Ona, who was still a teenager. He gets a job at Brown's and starts working under miserable conditions, along with thousands of others. Now, remember, he speaks little English, has little to no skills and yet, those evil meatpackers give him a job. Why did he stay? If it was so miserable, why didn't he leave?"

"Well, he couldn't leave, he had a family to support…" my teacher replied warily.

"No, you don't understand what I'm asking. The point I'm making is that he did find employment. He *chose* to go to Brown's. He also chose to remain at Brown's. He was even able to save some money for a down payment on a home. As far as his family's struggles, doesn't everybody struggle when they first start out in life?"

"Yes, but the working conditions at the plant were inhuman…"

"To you! To you they seem inhuman because you're a teacher! Tens of thousands of workers did those dirty jobs and tens of thousands were there to replace them if they left. To those people, those jobs and those conditions were better than other alternatives otherwise they would have gone somewhere else. Didn't Rudkus find another job later in the book in a fertilizer plant – again, speaking little English, with no skills and even with a criminal record? Did it ever occur to you, reading this book, that his life in Lithuania would have been worse than in Chicago, that his choices showed a preference?"

"That might be true, Mr. Giordano, but still, the harsh conditions were everywhere."

"You keep focusing on the harsh conditions, but would you agree with me that Brown's was not a prison, that nobody was forced to work there, or stay in Chicago, at gunpoint?"

"Okay, I'll give you that. But what you're missing is that the workers stayed because they were compelled to. They made just enough to keep themselves fed and housed but not enough to improve their conditions."

"I disagree. Doesn't everyone work to feed and house themselves? The fact that they were working to feed and house themselves is better than not working and starving on a park bench. That in itself is an improvement. Besides, didn't Rudkus make enough to save some of his money for his house?"

"Well, Mr. Giordano, supporting one's self and wage slavery are two, different things…"

"With all due respect, I'm saying that there is no such thing as wage slavery. A slave has no choices of his own. His labor is taken from him against his will with the threat of violence, not with the threat of a wage. We may be dependent upon a wage, but since we have free choice, we cannot be a slave to it. Isn't this the case with factory workers? They cannot be slaves to a wage unless they wish to be, just like anyone else who is dependent upon his salary to survive. They may not like what they are paid, they may think they are worth more, but they can always look for another job that will pay them more, if their skills warrant it."

The teacher thought a moment and said, "What I'm saying is that it was very difficult for these people to leave the situations they were in. It wasn't easy to get out from under their conditions."

"So, let me see if I understand what you're telling me. Rudkus made that huge effort to get there from Lithuania, made that long trip across the Atlantic Ocean from Europe, and then crossed half of the United States to get to Illinois. Are you telling me he couldn't have made the much smaller effort to hop onto a steamboat down the Mississippi or cross Lake Michigan, that he couldn't take a train ride or even a bicycle to any other place? It seems to me that all it would've taken was a decision to do so."

"Sometimes it's not as easy as that…"

"Well, I can give you an example from my own family. I'm the grandson of immigrants on both sides. My mother's father came to this country from Calabria when he was just a year older than I am now. He travelled with his older brother from Italy to the Chambersburg section of Trenton. He had cousins there that found him a job within a week of his arrival. After working there for a time, he and his brother thought they could do better elsewhere, so they moved to South Philly. Nobody stopped them from leaving Trenton and nobody stopped them from entering Philly. After a few more years, he was pretty much settled, got married to another immigrant woman from Italy, and had two children. His first wife died from a kidney infection. My grandmother had a similar experience. She had two children and was pregnant with a third when her husband died in the Spanish Flu epidemic. Since they were from the same town in Calabria and knew each other, my grandfather proposed. They were able to raise twelve children in a rowhome during the depression. My grandfather was a street cleaner in Philly. He spoke little English and had no formal education. My mother had to teach him how to sign his name. None of his children died in a mud puddle in the street. All of them finished high school. There were some tragedies along the way, but my grandfather would have told you that he could never have had in Italy what he had here."

"I'm sure that there are plenty of people, even in this

room, that are the descendants of immigrants who have stories similar to your grandparents. That still doesn't eliminate the fact that working conditions in those stockyards were harsh and that the workers suffered."

"Maybe so, but the story I just told you is of real people, not fictional characters from a novel. The fact that we're all here means that those who came before us didn't all die because they worked in harsh conditions. If the conditions were so bad and the immigrants were so mistreated, why did millions of them come here? I mean, do you think that after the first few thousand came and wrote back to the old country how bad the conditions were, millions of others from all over the world would still have followed anyway? Do you think they would've come here knowing they would be intentionally mistreated by evil business owners?"

"Well, Mr. Giordano, that's an interesting question, but I don't think we can get into the minds of those immigrants to know why they came here."

"We sure can, just ask! If they were anything like my grandparents, they'd tell you that any future here was better than no future back where they came from. So, it all comes down to making a choice and making the best of that choice. I do think, however, that there is one person responsible for all of the misery, illness, and death that the Rudkus family suffered in Chicago."

"Really, and whom would that be?"

"The author of the book..."

The teacher looked at me as though he was beginning to understand what I was inferring. Before he could comment though, the bell rang and the other students started to collect their books and other objects.

The teacher proclaimed above the noise, "We'll pick this up again on Monday. I'm curious to hear what else you have to say, Mr. Giordano."

"Okay, because there are still some things I'd like to add."

I had little to do over the weekend but I was eager to spend some time doing a bit of research into the effects of this book on American society during the turn of the century. I went with my father to the Camden County College campus, where he had some work to do, and spent about an hour and a half in their library. I got some help from the librarian looking up the bills that were enacted by Congress and signed into law by Teddy Roosevelt. Later, on the way home from the campus, I also asked my father about what he thought of the book and its consequences. I was surprised at the detailed response my father gave me. He not only knew the book, but the laws and federal agencies that were born from the supposed public outcry of its contents. He also knew that Sinclair was a dyed-in-the-wool communist with an agenda. He explained to me just who it was that benefitted from the legislation and that, in effect, consumers were actually less safe after the passing of the law. I took notes in the event I needed to give answers to my teacher.

My father looked at me a moment and said, "Tommy, I think it's a good thing that you want to do all of this research, but I have to tell you that it's enough that *you* know the truth. If you are doing all of this just to prove your teacher wrong, I think you'd be making a mistake."

"I don't want to prove him wrong. I already know he's wrong…"

"Well, by challenging him, you may win a battle but lose the war. You may make him an enemy and he's in a stronger position to do you harm than you are to defend yourself. Just be forewarned. I've been teaching a long time and I've seen all kinds of retaliations by teachers against students. He can make your life very hard."

"He was the one who said he wanted to continue the discussion we started yesterday. He asked what my opinion was. Should I not be honest about it and tell him what I think he wants to hear instead of what I really think?"

"No. There may come a time when that would be a good tactic, but I think you should say what you think. Just remember, some people take offense at differing opinions and think they are a personal affront. Just don't let it become that."

On Monday, the class began as usual. The other students were still settling down when the teacher began.

"Last Friday, we ended the class with Mr. Giordano giving us his opinion of *The Jungle*. Do you remember where we left off?"

"Yes. Basically, I said that the book was a comedy, that it was a fantasy and a pack of lies. We also talked about immigrants coming to this country hoping for a better life than what they left in their home countries. I also said that what we may consider harsh work environments, they may have considered preferable to the alternatives and that those dirty jobs were prized and sought after. Otherwise they would have sought opportunities somewhere else…"

"That's right. You also said that the one person responsible for all of their misery was Sinclair. That's an interesting statement. I'd like to know what you mean by that."

"That's easy. This book is not a documentary nor is it an investigative report. It's a novel. Sinclair could have simply changed the plot at any point of this fantasy and the characters could have gone in different, more positive directions. The author pre-determined all of this misery to prove a point that was only real in his mind because that's what he wanted the readers to believe was true. The way I see it, Sinclair gave his characters everything but free will; their actions are just not believable."

"Well, you know, Sinclair did go and work undercover in the slaughterhouse for seven weeks doing research. He saw with his own eyes what he wrote about."

"He needed seven weeks to research what, that slaughterhouses stink and that there is dirty work to be done? Think about it. We don't need to go to a sewage plant for seven weeks to know that the job stinks. I think that Sinclair set this book in the most disgusting industry he could think of because he already had an idea of what the conditions were before he went undercover. He saw exactly what he wanted to see. His only real research was to see the procedures of the operations and to learn the buzz words of the business. I also think that he created the conditions in his book to make everyone fail and to blame it all on capitalism. I mean, is it possible that, at every turn, Rudkus' family had a black cloud over them where they got hurt on the job, died from every imaginable cause, got eaten by rats, got raped, became prostitutes, hobos and beggars to survive? This was all designed to pull on the heart-strings of the reader to reinforce Sinclair's hatred for capitalism."

"Yes, he hated capitalism, but I believe he had good reasons and the book, through its plot, illustrated them."

"Even though all of the illustrations to prove it were lies? He never even defines what capitalism is. He merely associates it with greed. In fact, I think he confuses capitalism for greed. Would you say that greed only exists in capitalist economies? That it only came into existence with capitalism? I don't think so."

Another student asserted, "But what about that guy that fell into the meat grinder and was turned into a sausage? Don't you think that's pretty bad, Tom?"

"You mean lard, Janet, not a sausage. It sounds horrible. Too bad it never happened."

"How do you know it never happened?" she asked.

"Janet, think about it. How come there is no plaque with the guy's name on it? I mean, if something that horrible really happened, don't you think it would have been reported in the newspapers? It would have been headline news all over the United States. Why didn't Sinclair even have the decency to name the guy? Don't you think someone would have missed him when he

UNALIENABLE

didn't show up for work the next day? Besides, was the guy working nude? Don't you think his clothing and shoes would have bound up the grinder way before his mangled body got to the rendering tank? Do you really think any company would have continued their processing knowing that the fastest way to have their sales plummet is for news to get around that some consumer found Stanislav's big toe, his earlobe, and a couple of his molars in their lard?"

This got a laugh from the class. Even the teacher tried to hide his smile.

I continued, "I know it never happened because Teddy Roosevelt sent a couple of guys to investigate the claims made in the book and they gave him a report. The book caused such an uproar that he was forced to see if Sinclair was telling the truth. Even they reported that it was a pack of lies. They found no evidence of anybody ever getting killed and turned into lard or any other meat product."

The teacher asked, "Do you have the name of that report?"

"Yes. It's called the Neill-Reynolds Report."

"Where did you find this?"

"I did some research at the Camden County College library on Saturday."

"You actually went to the library to research this?"

"Yes, I did. I had only a gut feeling that this was a bunch of hogwash but had no real proof. I just couldn't believe that people who read this book took it for truth when it is only a fiction. It did create a public outcry and a whole bunch of politicians got on the bandwagon to do something."

"Well, I have to tell you that I'm impressed with your efforts. I haven't often seen someone look deeper into an argument like that on his own. Would you like to tell us all what you found out?"

"Yes, but first I have one more thing to say about immigrants. The reason that I knew that this book was hogwash from the onset is because of something my father once told me. He said that when people vote with their feet, they never do it to worsen their conditions. They do it to seek to better them. Coming from the misery and poverty of Europe, just the fact that they got work was a godsend to them. We may look at those dirty jobs and horrible workplaces and be disgusted, but we never ask what the alternatives were for those people. We can't imagine how they could be happy doing what we would never consider doing. Also remember, they could have left those jobs any time they wanted to."

"Fair enough…"

"Okay, so putting aside the characters and the plot of this book, what was it that Sinclair was trying to say? I can only see four things. The first is that capitalism is bad. The second is that the workers are being exploited by the business owners. The third is that the slaughterhouses were producing dangerous products that were placing the public's health at risk because of unsanitary conditions at the plants, and the fourth is that socialism has the answers to these supposed problems. Would you agree with this?"

"Put that way, yes."

"Okay. Now, I'd like to talk about each point in order. The first thing we should do is define capitalism. Most people use the word but have no idea what it is they are talking about."

"How would you define it?"

"Well, it is a voluntary, economic system where the means of production are invested in and owned by private individuals or corporations, which are collections of private individuals. The key ideas here are voluntary and privately owned and not owned or operated by a state or a government."

"Okay. So, what you're saying is that private people are investing their own money into their businesses…"

"Yes, they are *freely* investing their own money. Now, money is not capital; money is a resource. Capital is any other resource that money will buy to improve the productivity and efficiency of any operation. They are the tools and machines and things that companies can buy to reduce physical labor while increasing the output of their service or products. Investment in capital provides workers with new jobs, gives them better environments to work in, and reduces their physical workloads."

"Okay, but don't you think that this can also be the basis of greed that Sinclair wrote about?"

"Again, do you think there is no greed in socialist countries? Do you think there is no capitalism under socialism or communism? The only difference is in who is doing the investing and where the money comes from.

Under those regimes, committees or ministries are investing their people's monies into the means of production. Here, *individuals* are *voluntarily* investing their own money for a return on their investments. It costs *us* nothing. As I said, they create jobs, improve working environments, and increase wages while reducing prices for what they are making. Besides, why should I care if the owners of the factory who made this shirt are greedy if their greed produces a higher quality shirt that I can buy for less? Don't we all also benefit by their greed?"

The teacher, who was standing, looked at me with a slightly puzzled look on his face, leaned back, and sat on his desk.

I continued, "You see, as long as I have a choice in what I buy and nobody forces me to buy something I don't want, why would I care what a person's motives were for making a better shirt at a lower price? Now, if my money were taken from me by a government and thrown into making a product I don't want or need, I'm paying for it anyway."

"I think I see what you're trying to say…"

Another student chimed in and said, "Well, I don't like greedy people. I would never buy something from someone like that."

"Really? When you go shopping for shoes or anything else, are you telling me that you look for the most expensive products to buy? When you try to spend less for something or buy things that are on sale, aren't you being greedy? Besides, what is greed anyway? Most people would associate it with money, but isn't it really just people following their own interests and desires? You know what I think? I think that there isn't a single thing in this classroom, anything that we are wearing, hell even the building we are sitting in, that isn't a product of capitalism! If you were to boycott every company that operates to make a profit, you'd be standing naked in a field with dirty hair, dying of hunger."

"Alright. I can see you are making some good points. Please continue."

"Let's take the meatpacking industry itself. It was like a beehive of activity. It was mechanized like an assembly line. What was the reason for that? When my grandfather was in Italy, he never even saw a steak, let alone ate one. The best he could do, as far as meat was concerned, was chicken or rabbit, maybe some pork or horsemeat, and even more rarely some lamb on the holidays. Beef was so expensive that not even the nobility saw much of it on their tables. Here in America, beef, as well as every other meat product, was so cheap that even he, as a street cleaner, could buy some anytime he wanted. The meatpacking industry was supplying a huge demand and their competitive activities brought down the costs so much that practically anyone could buy it – even the people working in the plants producing those products. That is the result of private capitalism. But rather than continue on the good things that capitalism has given us, I'd like to just say that I completely disagree with Sinclair that capitalism is bad."

"Mr. Giordano, I'm sure you would come up with a good argument for your positive opinions of private capitalism. I'm not saying that I would agree, but I do have to admit that I also saw no definition for it."

"Well, the way I read this book, Sinclair's claim was that he was concerned for the distress of the workers, but to me this was overshadowed by his hatred for capitalism. I'll get back to this later though, because I found out some pretty interesting things about the political reaction to this book and it didn't go the way Sinclair had planned."

"Really? I'd be interested to hear this…"

"So, as far as the workers go, we've already gone over what I think about that. They chose the work they did…"

"Even so, don't you think the owners could have done something to improve the environment their employees were working in?"

"Are we sure that they hadn't already? Do we know what it was like to work in the stockyards and slaughterhouses twenty years before 1906? Is there a way to make the messy job of killing, gutting, and dressing animals a pleasant experience even today? Some jobs are just nasty, but someone has to do them if we want to eat a cheesesteak that won't cost us a month's salary. Another thing I'd like to add is that many of these industries were started by individuals or families who were doing the same thing on a smaller scale. In other words, the 'evil owners' enlarged their personal activities and by doing that, provided the very jobs that Sinclair complains about. If he was so concerned about

UNALIENABLE

the workers being exploited in the slaughterhouses in Chicago, why wasn't his solution to start one, improve the conditions as he saw fit in his own plant, and increase the pay scale for his own employees? Let me put it this way: if I buy a house next to a smelly trash dump and find that the stench bothers me, I can't complain because I knew before I bought the house that it was next to a dump. Can't I say the same thing about a job?"

"I see your point. You're saying that, in all fairness, the job is what it is."

"Exactly."

"So, now what about the sanitary conditions? Do you have anything to say about them? Don't you think it was a good thing for the government to step in and regulate their activities under the laissez faire economy?"

"Here is where it gets interesting. Sinclair gives you the impression that the meatpacking industry was under no control at all. This is complete bunk. This industry was under strict control by the state governments where they were located. There were standards that required spot meat inspections on a frequent basis. If those standards were not met, the plant was shut down until they were. They would lose money! It was in the interest of the owners to comply and keep their products safe for the public. Besides, even if there weren't any controls, haven't we been hunting and eating meat for thousands of years without a government inspector standing next to us to see how we gut, dress, and prepare it for storage? If a person was so concerned about the quality of the meat from one source, couldn't he simply buy it from another? I'm a Roman Catholic but I would not hesitate buying kosher meats if I thought they were safer. I would be assured that a Rabbi would not pass a product that would harm the people it was intended for. This is how a free market works so, no, I don't think the government should have interfered."

"Well, I'm not too sure I agree with you on this point. It is the purpose of governments to protect their citizens, don't you think?"

"Of course, I do. That's why we have courts of law. Anybody can bring a company to court and sue them for damages and the courts would issue injunctions against the company to cease their operations until the problem was corrected. It would be in the company's best interests to comply with the laws or else they would lose money. There was no need for federal laws to interfere. Do you remember the laws that were passed because of this book?"

"If I'm not mistaken, it was a meat inspection law."

"One of them. On Saturday, I read that there were two laws. One was called The Meat Inspection Act and the other was called The Pure Food and Drug Act. The second one led to the creation of a government agency called The Bureau of Chemistry. This turned into the Food and Drug Administration sometime later. Meat inspection now is under the USDA."

"Well, I see you really did do your homework! I was only partly aware of all of this. But you do see that this book had an effect on our country."

"Oh, it did have three effects and not one of them was

positive."

"What do you mean?"

"This is the really interesting part of this story. Guess who were the biggest lobbyists for these laws?"

"I wouldn't know. Who?"

"The owners of the slaughterhouses!"

"Oh, come on! Are you telling me these people pushed for laws against their own interests?"

"Who said they were against their interests? In fact, it was a big score for them."

"How could that be?"

"Do you remember we talked about those state regulations? Every time the meat inspectors came to the plant, the company being inspected had to foot the bill. These laws passed that expense onto the citizens because the inspectors became federal employees paid with our taxpayer's money, even if that taxpayer doesn't eat meat! On top of this, who do you think the politicians asked to create the federal regulations for meat inspection? That's right, the people from the industry who knew the ins and outs of animal inspection – the owners of the plants doing the slaughtering. The result was that the federal standards were less strict than the state standards and, since the federal laws trump state laws in this case, this meant that their products could be sold following standards that were less safe than before. It also increased consumer confidence in their products by deception because of a federal seal of approval. And one more thing: meat prices increased. In 1905 and '06, beef was about ten cents a pound. In 1907, after the law was enacted, it went up to fifteen cents. After all, didn't it have a federal seal of approval on it? Would you call these things positive? It also doesn't seem to bother anyone that the FDA, which is responsible for approving drugs and medicines to enter the market, was born from the same pack of lies!"

The teacher placed his hand over his mouth and stared at me. He was at a loss for words. The other students started talking amongst themselves while I sat waiting for the teacher to say something. I could not tell whether he was angry, embarrassed, or amused.

I added, "You see, the politicians were all beating their chests telling the People how they stuck it to those evil, greedy capitalist owners when it was actually the People who got shafted. The meatpackers laughed all the way to the bank. Can you now see who really benefited? My father once told me that you should never look at the supposed good intentions of any act but at its consequences. What are the effects?"

The teacher removed his hand and I could see a smile. He rubbed his eyes and asked, "Do you have any other surprises for me Mr. Giordano?"

"Yes, I do. I just have one more thing to add. Did you notice that the only laws enacted dealt with food safety and sanitation, and nothing was passed for the conditions of the workers? There was a reason for that. I think the American people understood that this book was a load of crap and so did the politicians. The public reaction was for the sanitary questions, even though they were completely exaggerated, and the politicians had to jump onto anything they could write a law for. Sinclair intended the book to create an outcry for the 'exploited workers' but it didn't. Americans were smarter than that and saw his agenda for what it was. In the end, he failed and he wasn't happy about it."

The teacher cleared his throat and addressed the class, "After hearing what Mr. Giordano just said, how many of you have changed your minds about what you initially thought about this book?"

Most of the students raised their hands, which surprised me. There was some back and forth between some of the students and the teacher. I got the distinct impression that he was watching his own convictions being shattered and he looked at me while responding to an ever-increasing barrage of questions. I sat there disinterested.

The class eventually ended. As I was putting my things together to leave, the teacher approached me and asked me what my next period class was, and I told him it was lunch and then recreation after that. He asked me to give him a few minutes and waited until the other students had gone and we were alone. I was surprised when he addressed me by my first name.

"You want to know something, Tom? I've been teaching high school for six years now and I have never had anyone challenge me on Sinclair. I have to say that this was the most stimulating class that I can remember teaching. While I was listening to you, it struck me that you don't think or speak like a fifteen-year-old. Why haven't you ever contributed like this to classroom discussions before?"

"Most of the things that you present in class I disagree with, so I keep my mouth shut."

"Well, Tom, I can accept a different point of view. And I have to say that you've taught me something during the last two classes. I'll never look at Sinclair the same way again."

"It was not my intention to take that away from you. I didn't enter into the discussion to convince anyone of anything. It's not my place. I gave you my views because you asked me. Most of the things people think and say they sincerely believe but they very rarely examine. They are free to believe anything they want to. Please don't be offended, but you have a tendency to present things in a way that convinces the other students that there is something good about socialism. I was raised to see things differently than that. My father taught me of the evils of socialism and the crimes committed in its name."

The teacher looked at me and his eyebrows came together, leaving a sharp crease above the bridge of his nose. He seemed to be reflecting upon my words.

"Well, we got sidetracked in class and didn't get to this argument…"

"I know. You see, if I were teaching this class and had to discuss this book, I would not have hidden the fact that Sinclair was a known communist and that his book reflected his beliefs. You had a perfect opportunity to demonstrate how false propaganda could have an emotional effect upon a people and lead them to pass negative laws that end up benefitting small groups and hurting society. That is the biggest lesson to be learned, not its contents or what he wrote. This should have been the reason for exposing kids to Sinclair."

The teacher heard my words and his gaze dropped to the floor.

I continued, "Now, I'm just a kid and it's not for me to tell you how or what to teach, but my father has already exposed me to these things. He guided my reading and we've had long discussions. On many occasions, he made me realize that I was thinking with my heart and not my head. He told me that an ancient Greek philosopher once said to believe what your master says, but never swear by it. That is how I look at school."

"Your father sounds like an interesting person. One day I'd like to speak with him."

I smiled at him and said, "You already have!"

He smiled back, then asked, "What does he do?"

"He's a professor of Business Administration but also Economics."

"I see… Well, we still haven't talked about socialism in class. Would you be willing to discuss this next time if I asked you?"

"I can't refuse you if you ask, but don't you think the other students will get sick of hearing me talk?"

"Half of your classmates are asleep, and the other half only tell me what they think I want to hear. I'll ask if they have anything to add. Some of them seemed to wake up after your discussion, though. I'll make you a promise: I'll re-think what my opinions are on this subject."

"Are you sure I haven't offended you?"

"Not at all. I've always prided myself on having an open mind. It surprises me that you are only fifteen and have thought more deeply on this subject than I have. I think that you were more fortunate than I – my father was a bricklayer and we never had any meaningful discussions on anything other than cars or sports."

I sensed some embarrassment in his voice which I could not let pass. I don't really know the reason, but I asked him, "How long was your dad a bricklayer?"

"Let me think. More than 25 years, why?"

"Well, it means he's an honest man. He wouldn't have lasted long as a mason if he weren't. It also means he was good at what he did."

"I guess so. Yes, you're right."

"Did he fight in the war?"

"In Europe. He was in the Army."

"My Dad was a Sea Bee in the South Pacific."

"I see. Those were difficult times."

"Did you ever work with him?"

"Well, when I was a teenager and while I was in college, I did some summer work with him. It was heavy and dirty work, but satisfying."

"Did you learn anything from it?

"How do you mean?"

"What did you come away with after working with him?"

"Well, that I didn't want to do that work for the rest of my life."

"And now, you're a teacher."

UNALIENABLE

He looked at me as if he had come to a realization about what we had discussed in class. His eyes widened slightly and his mouth dropped. It made me smile.

"What about the importance of a good, level footing? Any unleveled footing of a half an inch will turn into a foot as the courses of bricks increase, right? Maybe that's why they say a level footing is true. I think your father taught you more than you want to realize."

I paused a moment because something had come to my mind. I continued, "You know, this just reminded me of a story my mom once told me. One day, she was walking home from school with some friends. As they turned the corner, she saw her father sweeping the street. Their eyes met and he called out to her to say hello. She ignored him and continued walking. When he finally arrived home from work, my mother went to him and told him not to greet her on the street if he sees her with her friends. She said she was embarrassed. She told me that she immediately saw that her choice of words hurt him. He told her, in broken English, that when he cleans the street, he pushes the dirt with his broom first, then puts his foot down, that his path was always clean before he stepped. His response brought tears to my mother's eyes."

My teacher gazed off into space for a moment, biting his lower lip. He then said softly, "You can go to lunch now. I'll see you next time. Oh, and Tom, give my compliments to your father; he made you wise before your time…"

I nodded my head and left him staring at the empty classroom. As I walked to the cafeteria, I realized just how much I was influenced by my father and his ordered, analytical approach to any argument. When I told him of the events of that day, he said I was fortunate that my teacher was relatively young and had an open mind about things. He told me that it was more likely that if he were older and more jaded after years of teaching, it probably would not have been a happy ending for me. My father then told me to give my teacher our phone number and tell him to call whenever he wanted. I don't think he ever did, but I can never be sure. My father would never have revealed it to me.

PART III

ECONOMICS

CHAPTER 12

HUMAN DESIRE, HUMAN CHOICE, HUMAN ACTION

When I was sixteen, I posed a number of questions for my father to answer. I don't actually recall which of these questions it was that I asked, but the discourse eventually turned to what motivates people to do the things they do. My father told me that the only thing that concerned him as to people's motivations was whether or not they were moral. All motivations, to him, were based in self-interest, though some of them he described as "enlightened" self-interest, which resulted in such things as charities, eleemosynary institutions, private universities and colleges, private hospitals, and clinics and museums, to name a few.

He also explained to me that the achievements of our human race were built upon individuals following their free will to pursue their own self-interests. As a result, mankind itself was the beneficiary. These ideas were not his, he told me, but were gleaned from the observations of a brilliant Scotsman named *Adam Smith* in the late 1700s. Smith was a moral philosopher and political economist of the Scottish Enlightenment and is considered to be the father of modern free-market economics. Smith's considerations on human action extend far beyond economics alone. My father told me that it appeared to him that Smith was simply applying an understanding of the rules of Natural Law to economics.

My father explained that he had read two of Smith's books, *The Theory of Moral Sentiments* and the *Inquiry into the Nature and Causes of the Wealth of Nations*. The *Wealth of Nations*, prophetically, was published in the same year as our Declaration of Independence – 1776 – and had a profound effect upon our Founding Fathers.

He went on to describe just how rational self-interest and competition can lead to economic prosperity.

To begin, he gave examples from history and how the so-called "robber barons" of the 1900s were nothing of the sort. He illustrated how their activities had far-reaching benefits to society because they lowered prices, increased wages for workers, provided new industries and jobs, and even staid off the extinction of the whales. Goods and services, in the competitive fields of the free market, became widely available, improved the living standards of millions and prompted a mass immigration from all over the world to our shores - even our own family followed the dream of a better life in America.

UNALIENABLE

To make the observation more personal, he gave my friend Frank's father as an example to provide further proof of his theory.

"Take Dr. Pettinelli as an example. Here is a man who was born into poverty and lost his father at a young age. After he was released from the Marine Corps, he decided he wanted to become a physician. This meant that he'd have to work and sacrifice to get through college, then through medical school. He was driven to fulfill his desire to become a doctor. Now, we don't know what stimulated him to do this, we only know that this was his motivation – perhaps he was seeking a financially secure activity to provide a particular life-style, perhaps it was the prestige the title commands, perhaps he wanted it because someone else told him he couldn't do it. We'll never know without asking him. However, what happened after he graduated and got his license to practice, we can objectively study.

I'm sure that his first few years in practice were difficult; they are for everyone. But eventually, he put enough money away to purchase the row-home on Ninth and Reed Streets to open his private practice. Now, here is where Smith's observations become clear. He had to renovate the ground floor. This required materials and labor. The materials, such as wood, came from the northwest of the U.S., the nails came from the steel mills in Pittsburgh, the sheetrock, windows, doors and everything related to the reconstruction came from other sources in other places. Take the nails, for example. The iron ore had to be mined. It had to be smelted and converted to steel using carbon, which also had to be either mined as coal or burned down from wood. The mining processes required the physical labor of men and the use of heavy equipment, produced in factories. Then there was the transport from the mines to the mills and from the mills to the factory to produce the nails and from that factory to the wholesalers and then to the retailers and then to the contractor for use in the remodeling. The transportation – trains and trucks – was all produced in factories which got their primary materials from different sources from all around the world, not just from the U.S. Are you beginning to see the complexity of just producing a nail? Literally hundreds of thousands of people from all around the world were involved and employed in what is known as the higher orders of production. Now, expand this to all of the other products and all of the other services, just for the building materials alone. Now, consider those laborers directly involved – the carpenters, the masons, the electricians, the plumbers, the plasterers, the finishers and painters and so on. Each of these received wages for their labor. And it doesn't stop there."

"Dr. Pettinelli," he continued, "had to furnish his office. He had to acquire office materials, from file folders to paper clips and staples. He had to purchase all of his medical equipment and examination tables, autoclaves for sterilization and on and on. Each of these things are produced the same way as all of the other materials in the renovation with tens, if not hundreds of thousands of people involved. And, it still doesn't stop there!"

"He had to hire a receptionist," my father went on, "He had to arrange a network of laboratory and specialist contacts for services beyond his competence. All of these benefited by his degree. And we must never forget his patients, all of which benefitted by his expertise. Dr. Pettinelli not only treats patients for a fee, but also, I'm sure, has seen many patients pro bono over the years."

"Now reflect upon that," my father instructed me. "It is so complex that it would be extremely difficult to organize and write it all down, let alone presume to control it. Probably millions of people benefitted from Dr. Pettinelli pursuing his private interests, including his own family."

There was another point my father wanted to make: there was no single person, or committee, or government agency involved in any of this activity. The individuals involved didn't know each other, lived in different countries, spoke different languages, had different religions, and had no idea where all of their efforts were going. Prices for their labors, services, and products were all communicated through this system based upon voluntary interactions and competition related to the allocation of those activities and resources. This mass of activity was based upon the mutual benefits each person perceived they were getting from their interactions.

This was Adam Smith's "invisible hand" at work. He further explained that this was why any centralized control would never work. Collectives are not of a single mind; no one or group, no matter what nice little economic models they conceive, could ever take into account all of the desires and all of the self-interests of the entire population of the earth and operate as efficiently as the invisible hand. Centralized control of the means of production or the division of labor – even a pricing mechanism – have produced, and will always produce, failures on a massive scale. No governmental body or commissar had ordered Dr. Pettinelli to become a doctor, just as nobody had ordered Henry Ford to create the assembly line or Edison to create the light bulb or Andrew Carnegie to revolutionize the steel industry and so on.

This was just another example of my father's views on how the expression of free will leads to human action for the benefit of society and why that expression is paramount to improving the lives of the people.

"Now, when you look at Dr. Pettinelli today, you see a wealthy, successful man. There are those who will never recognize the struggles he went through to attain what he has today. They will envy him his wealth, his success, and the respect he has from the people he serves and his colleagues. They will hate him for the house he lives in or the car he drives or the vacations he takes. The interesting thing is, even if the socialists take everything he has from him and divide it all up among the population, the only thing they would accomplish would be the gain of a fraction of a cent, if that, and the destruction of the services he provides and the benefit to the economy he has proven to be – to their own detriment!"

UNALIENABLE

"Never begrudge the honestly attained wealth or success of another," my father instructed. "Instead, try to imagine the benefit that person has been to society and the wealth his pursuits have provided to many, many others – just by his activities alone. It is not a zero-sum game. Dr. Pettinelli didn't become wealthy by making others poorer; by becoming wealthy himself, he enriched everyone around him."

CHAPTER 13

WHAT IS MONEY, DAD?

It was in the summer of 1965, and I was not yet 10 years old, when my father gave me my first lesson on money and economics as we sat under the maple tree in our back yard. He had just raised my weekly allowance to thirty-five cents and was eager to give me some basic instruction on the subject.

The conversation began as we discussed a Humphrey Bogart movie we had watched on TV the day before. It was called *The Treasure of the Sierra Madre* - a story of how the desire for gold could corrupt a man's soul and drive him to his own destruction. He told me a story of a couple of the men in his battalion during the war who saw killing the enemy as an opportunity to harvest the gold fillings in their teeth. He was not averse to souvenir hunting after the battles he was engaged in, but the act of opening a dead man's mouth and prying out the man's fillings or crowns, or smashing them out with a rifle butt, was beyond his sense of morality, even though, he admitted, morality was in short supply on those islands. Those two men made it through the war and returned home wealthier than my father could estimate, but he didn't know what happened to the men after that. He imagined that they either became very successful or wound up in prison – probably both.

I asserted, "I was told that money was the root of all evil."

"Who told you that, Tommy?"

"Father Flanagan."

"Well, Father Flanagan got it wrong. The saying is actually 'the **LOVE** of money is the root of all evil,' but even this is a false notion. I'm not sure where this idea came from, but it was probably from those who have no money and want to justify their failures to get it and foment hate against others for their success in making it. Anyway, evil has been around a lot longer than money has been. People are motivated by their own self-interests. Sometimes it is the desire for money, sometimes it's the desire for postage stamps, butterflies, baseball cards, works of art, books, guns, or automobiles. People place value on and covet millions of different things – including other people. There is nothing as strong as the destructive power of love itself or jealousy. The actual root of all evil is the desire of a few to control others – to have and exert power over them without their consent. That's why we fought the war against the socialists in Germany and Italy and the imperialists in Japan. In any case, money is neither good nor bad – it just is what it is and it is a very useful commodity."

"What is money, anyway? I mean, I know that it is dollars and cents and all that, but where did it come from?"

"Those are two questions that have very long answers, Tommy. Although money is the translation of your time or labor into a physical commodity, it is best defined simply as a medium of exchange. Now, what do I mean by that? There was a time when people traded or bartered the things that they had for the things that they wanted from other people. Let's say that we were both farmers and I grew wheat and you grew corn. We, as sellers, would set the value of one bushel of our produce at what we believed our produce to be worth. Of course, we, as buyers, would determine what the other guy's produce was worth to us. We would then come to an agreement as to how many bushels of wheat was equal to a bushel of corn. We would call this a direct exchange because we are dealing with only two people. Obviously, if we were to trade these goods, we couldn't walk around with them in our pockets. When our harvests came in, we would bring them to a silo for storage and the owner of the silo would give us a note indicating how much of our product we have in his facility, minus his fee for the use of the silo. So, instead of trading the physical bushels, we could trade the notes, or write up a note ourselves to tell the silo operator how much to give the buyer. These silo notes then act as a medium of exchange and, for all intents and purposes, can circulate around as money. If I go, let's say, to the barber, he may ask me for a quarter of a bushel for a haircut, but then he'd have to find someone who would take his note for a quarter bushel for other things that he'd like to buy. We would then call this an indirect exchange because there are more than two people involved. As the number of products and services in society become too numerous to barter, and the exchanges become more and more complicated and time consuming, a proper medium of exchange becomes necessary. In order to facilitate these indirect exchanges, the medium has to have what is called an intrinsic value in and of itself. If it is a metal, such as gold or silver, its purity, or assay, and its weight must be determinable by specific, universal standards. A specific weight of the metal then becomes the standard value by which all other products and services are compared. These are much easier to carry around and they become the middle part of any exchange in goods and services. In other words, I give you money for your product and you take that money and purchase another's product or services. The unfortunate thing is that the transactions then can also be more easily taxed."

"Why gold, Dad? Why is gold so valuable?"

"As I said, for its intrinsic value. That is to say it is rare to come by and it has a value to industry. It's used in electronics, in dentistry, and making jewelry, for example. It has a long shelf-life in that it doesn't corrode, it can't be destroyed by fire or water and it will last forever. Additionally, its value is due to its difficulty to obtain and as long as the gold that leaves the reserves for use in industry is replaced at the same rate that comes in

UNALIENABLE

from new mining, it is not subject to large fluctuations in purchasing value. Also, it can't be counterfeited. As a commodity, it is a perfect medium of exchange. If we decided to use something like corn as the medium, its value would be time-limited; it could rot before you could spend it and its use and value to the market would vanish."

"Why aren't we still using gold as money then?"

"Well, our constitution still requires gold and silver to be the only currencies. The government's only role in this is to guarantee the purity of the metals and their weights. The federal government was to have no power to print money, only to coin it. It has always been known that when governments have the power to print money, they will run the printing presses to excess, devaluing the purchasing power of the currency. The first example that I know of in America happened up in Massachusetts back in the 1690s. There was a failed raid on the French up in Canada and the attackers came back empty-handed. There was no plunder to be sold in the markets and the soldiers couldn't be paid. The colonial government came up with the idea that they could print up some pound notes to be redeemed at a later time with coin – what is called 'specie.' The government promised that this was only to be done once and never repeated, but when the government saw no immediate ill-effects, they went from the initial 7,000 pounds, and, within a short time, printed up another 40,000 pounds. The problem was, though, that the people distrusted the government to redeem these notes and started to discount them to about

40% of their face value in trade. People also began to hoard the coins, which had real value, and only used the notes in commerce. Coinage in circulation then became scarce. Obviously, prices for goods went up because the market value of the paper pounds was only 40% of the hard currency pounds. The government then tried to force the people to accept these notes at their face value, passing 'legal tender' laws. Other colonies started to do the same and trade and money wars followed between the colonies. You see, commodity money has a value set by the market, just as any other commodity. When the government comes in and sets a value to something, either above or below the market values, problems will always follow and people will find ways to protect their own interests. But, to get back to your question, we no longer use gold in daily commerce because the federal government under FDR forced it out of use back in 1933."

"Why did he do that?"

"Well, the reasons are too complicated to explain to you right now. Let's just say that there were those in government and some respected economists who believed that this was one way to allow the government, through the Federal Reserve System, to pump more money into the economy and help lower interest rates for businesses to stimulate job growth during the Depression. At least, these were two of the major reasons they gave. I think it was a lot of hogwash, but this is another subject altogether and a little too detailed to talk about now. Just remember that the truest, real value of any product or service should be based in its gold value equivalent."

"You mean what something is worth in gold?"

"Yes, that's right."

"How do you figure that out?"

"All you have to do is look at the dollar equivalent of an ounce of gold. You can tell what's happening to the value of the dollar by how many of them it takes to buy an ounce of gold over time. I'll give you an example. Let's imagine that George Washington gave one of your ancestors a dollar back in 1776. At the time, you could buy an ounce of gold for about $20.00. That dollar had the same buying power all the way until 1933 when FDR took us off of the gold standard and raised the price of an ounce of gold to about $35.00 the next year. The same thing you could have bought for a dollar in 1776 and again in 1876 will now cost you $1.57. Most people would look at this and say the price of the product or service has gone up but this is not the case; the value of the dollar has gone down."

"I get that! If the dollar is worth less and the value of the thing that I want to buy stays the same, then I have to give more money for it."

"Well, now you understand what inflation means. You see, as the government keeps asking the Federal Reserve to print up dollars and pump them into circulation, the more the buying power of the dollar decreases and the more dollars it takes to buy something. We now know that it takes about a year and a half before the effects of these additions to circulating money are felt. This means that the government, at the time the Federal Reserve receives the order for the money, has the benefit of that day's buying power because the dollar's decrease in value won't take effect until eighteen months later, which will be reflected in increased prices. On top of this, the money is created out of thin air at the time of the loan to the government and must be paid back with interest by the taxpayers. The other thing to consider is that we now operate under what's called a fractional reserve banking system, meaning that the banks are only obligated to keep about one tenth of the money they lend on hand to prevent runs on the banks by depositors."

I pondered this a moment and said, "That doesn't make any sense to me."

"How do you mean?"

"Well, if I put $100.00 in the bank and they lend out $90.00 of it, where does the money come from if I want it back?"

"You're not the only depositor. Other people's money will cover your deposit. However, if everyone wants their money at the same time, then it becomes a problem. This is why the Federal Reserve was supposedly created – to provide reserves to counter the bank runs. During the Depression, however, it intentionally didn't do what it was created to do. It failed miserably when put to the test. The '29 Depression lasted until well after the Second World War, most probably because of the government's intrusions into the market and attempts to stimulate things that needed no stimulation. In fact, many economists claim the war ended the Depression because of the increased production for the war effort, but this is also just more hogwash. It was really only a false recovery masked by the war economy and then the European and Asian reconstruction afterwards. There was another, more devastating depression in 1920 and the government did absolutely nothing, which is what it should do, and that cleared up in one year, simply by allowing the market to react and adjust with no government intervention. However, let's stick to the original discussion. Those in government have taken us off of the gold standard and are now planning to debase our silver currency as well. What do you think this means?"

I thought a moment and then figured it out, much to my father's surprise.

"What it tells me is that the coins are going to have their weight in silver reduced because they are actually worth more than their face value, like a quarter has the silver that is actually worth around thirty cents."

"Exactly! You've got it."

"Dad, when you were talking about swapping bushels of wheat for corn and said that we couldn't put them in our pockets, I was just thinking the same thing about silver dollars. They each weigh about an ounce. They can get pretty heavy to carry around if you have enough of them. Aren't the paper dollars easier to carry?"

"Sure. But there are a few things you have to consider about paper dollars. The first thing is trust; they are subject to devaluation, as we've just talked about. The other thing to think about is where they come from.

There was a time when the U. S. Treasury printed up these paper dollars with an exact backing in either gold or silver, which meant you could take them to a bank and have them redeemed for their value in those metals. In other words, they couldn't print up more notes than the amount of gold or silver that backed them. By law, they had to be redeemed at the demand of the holder of the paper. These are called Treasury Notes. Silver Certificates are still around, but the way things are going, they'll be eliminated completely in the near future. These have now been replaced with Federal Reserve Notes, which are merely promissory notes or 'IOU's' from a private banking system. They are basically not backed by anything other than a promise to pay, but they don't specify what it is they'll pay. A dollar has no value set to it because real money is actually based upon a weight of some commodity. Those in government seem to believe that money is anything the government says it is, but markets don't work that way. Promises have no real value and, as far as governments are concerned, don't last longer than the breath it takes to make them."

"Why hasn't the government printed more? I mean, who decides when to stop printing fake dollars?"

"Well, there is still a check on how much the Federal Reserve can print up. Our international trade still has the dollar linked to gold. We can't just continue to devalue the money without creating international repercussions. You know, after the First World War, Germany was forced to pay back reparations to the countries that it had fought, but the payback was impossible. They printed up so much money that they ran out of paper. People took their wages home in wheelbarrows and had to spend it as fast as they got it because sometimes, in a matter of hours, their money lost its value. On the other hand, there were two economies in our history that had no inflation for over eight-hundred years – the Eastern Holy Roman Empire and the Kingdom of Naples."

"Why is that?"

"Because in both cases, their governments were forbidden from printing money. This was the way our government was supposed to act; it was to have no influence on the markets or the production of money. In colonial times, the British government didn't even allow mints to exist here and we used other countries' money as currency – the Spanish Pieces of Eight or the Austrian Maria Theresas, for example. Their governments were trusted to assure that the coins were of optimal assay and of the proper weight. In fact, we still have terms for coinage from those days. Since the Spanish dollar could be physically divided into eight pieces with a chisel and a hammer, two bits of it was equal to a quarter of a dollar. Have you ever heard someone call a quarter '*two bits*?'"

"Yes, but I didn't know where it came from. Dad, you said that there was a time when money wasn't around and people swapped things. How can there be an economy without money?"

"Economies aren't necessarily based upon the flow of money. I would say that economies are based more upon human desire than money."

"Human desire? I don't understand what you mean."

"Do you remember what I told you about people pursuing their own self-interests?"

"Yes."

"What are self-interests if not personal desires? It is from here that economies are born – at the individual level. In any case, in order to answer your question, there are a few definitions we need to consider. Firstly, we have to define 'economy.' Do you know what the word means?"

I had heard the word lots of times, but never really bothered to look it up. As a consequence, I really couldn't put into words what the actual meaning was. He told me to think about it for a moment while he went into the house for a cup of coffee. I knew that this usually meant that I was in for a more detailed lesson.

CHAPTER 14

ECONOMICS EXPLAINED

My father returned to the picnic table and sat down with his mug of coffee.

"Well?" he asked.

"I tried to think about it but didn't get anywhere."

"Tommy, don't feel bad. I know plenty of adults who think they know the meaning, but really don't. The word comes from the Greek '*oikos,*' meaning 'house,' and '*nemein,*' meaning '*to manage.*' So, the basic definition is 'household managing' or 'household management.' Of course, the word has taken on a more complex meaning today and is best defined as the 'judicious use of wealth and resources.' Now, this applies to individuals and families, as well as to businesses and governments. In fact, it applies to all life forms. Okay, so before we go further, think of the words in the definition and we'll define them in turn to get at the full meaning of economics. Let's start with 'wealth' and 'resources.'

DR. THOMAS V. GIORDANO

What is 'wealth?'"

I responded, "Money."

"Are you sure it's just money?"

By his asking the question, I knew that my answer was not totally correct, but I didn't know what else to add.

"Okay, the proper definition of wealth is the net worth of a person, household, business or nation, meaning the value of all assets owned minus all of the liabilities owed at any point in time. Now, can you tell me what 'assets' and 'liabilities' are?"

"You once told me that an asset was anything that puts money into my pocket and a liability was anything that took it out of my pocket."

"Very good, that's right. An asset is either something you own or something that earns you an income, and a liability is a debt or something you owe. Well, wealth is defined exactly by this, what you own minus what you owe. Can you see that not all assets are money? Anything you own that has a value to someone else is considered an asset. I'll tell you what, empty your pockets on the table."

I did so. Before us lay thirty-five cents, a pocketknife, a pack of chewing gum, and a small magnifying glass.

"Now, what are these?"

"Assets?"

"Yes. Now, can you think of anything else?"

"Well, Bobby Poolos wanted to trade me something for my Phillies cap."

"So, your Phillies cap is also an asset. So are your clothes and your sneakers. You get the point?"

"Yeah. As long as I have something that someone else

may want, it is my asset."

"Anything else? Think about it.

I wasn't quite sure what he was trying to get at and I told him so.

"What about you? You have a brain and two hands, aren't your abilities an asset?

"Can people be assets?"

"They sure can. Your labor and your intellect are also your assets. Now, do you owe anything to anyone?"

"No, but Bobby owes me a nickel that I lent him to buy some gum."

"No, no, I'm looking for *your* liabilities, not Bobby's. But what he owes you is still your asset. You still own the nickel that Bobby borrowed and spent, but let's not get off the subject at hand. So, you don't owe anything to anybody?

"No, I don't."

"Good. Now, if people can be assets, they can also be liabilities. You see, to me, you and your brothers are liabilities, in the strictest sense. I feed, clothe, and support you. I have to educate you, keep you healthy, and make sure there is a roof over your heads. As your father, my objective is to guide you towards being independent men and to make sure that you become thinking citizens and assets to our society. Now, you shouldn't think of yourself as a liability to me since we are bound by blood. We tend to think of ourselves as individuals, but we are really a family unit, which is the basis of society. As you grow older and you can contribute more and more to the survival of the family, you become more and more of an asset. Anyway, let's get back to the discussion. Now, we know the definition of economy. We know what the terms 'wealth,' 'assets,' and 'liabilities' mean. What about 'resources?'"

I couldn't add anything and waited for him to continue.

"In economics, a resource is defined as a service or an asset used to produce goods and other services that meet human needs and wants. There are basically two kinds of resources – human and non-human. When we talk about human resources, we are referring to a person's labor, expertise, skills, or management abilities to reach a desired goal. In other words, any human ability or activity that can be utilized to provide a service or a product. Do you understand this idea?"

"I think so."

"Okay, now let's see. We have a lawn that needs regular mowing. The objective is to maintain the yard in order. If I ask you to mow the lawn, what are you?"

I immediately understood where he was going with his question. "I'm your resource."

"Very good. You become an employable asset and resource. Even though I am able to mow the lawn, I could employ your labor to do this chore for me. This frees up time that I could use more productively elsewhere. It is worth it to me to pay you because my time is worth more than yours. So you see, when you are sitting around and not doing anything to enhance the survival of our family, you are a liability with the potential to be a resource. When you are actively doing chores and helping out around the house, you become a resource."

"Dad, when Eddie and I were too young to mow the lawn, that teenager Neil came over to do it. I remember that you paid him more than you give to me or Eddie. How come he got more than we do?"

"Neil was one of my students and he worked during the summers cutting lawns. When he came over, he brought his own lawnmower. He had his own gasoline. He had to drive over here with his pick-up truck and he took away the clippings. You see, I was not only paying for his labor but also the use of his assets and the service of disposing of the grass. When you cut the lawn, you're using my lawnmower, my gas, my rake, and my trash bags for the clippings. This means that the only asset you are contributing is your labor. Do you see the difference?"

My father continued, "Now, how about *non-human* resources? Can you tell me what they are?"

"I think it would be something like tools and machines. Maybe land and money?"

"You're on the right track, but it is much more than that. We are talking about physical goods that can be used as primary materials for industry as well as anything that can increase efficiency and productivity. Also, there are natural resources, such as water, minerals, metals, oil, coal, and other energy sources to run the machinery. You get the idea?"

"Yeah."

"Okay, now let's review again. We know what wealth is. We know what assets and liabilities are. We now know how two kinds of resources are defined. Now, what about the term 'judicious use.' What do you think this means?"

"Well, 'judicious' means judging something."

"Okay, to judge something. How about if we expand that definition to 'an ability for reaching wise or just decisions?' Does this make sense to you?"

"Yeah."

"Alright. Now, how do you arrive at a wise decision? What I mean to say is, what do you base your decisions upon to determine whether they are wise or not?"

I paused for a moment and said that decisions had to be based on facts. He agreed, but went on to say that this was not enough. Facts only have a value if they are considered against something else.

My father went on, "Let's go back to mowing the lawn. Imagine that I dedicate $3.00 a month to cut the lawn once a week. We'll call this our 'lawn budget.' Now, a while ago we said that the purpose for cutting the lawn was to keep the yard in order, right? Keeping the yard in order is then our mission or objective. The $3.00 is used to purchase things like gasoline and oil for the lawnmower. It goes for maintenance of the machine as well. It also goes for the purchase of bags for the clippings. Would it be a wise decision if I went out and bought baseball cards with some of the money that I budgeted for the lawn care?"

"No."

"Why not?"

"Because you can't cut the grass with baseball cards."

"That's right. The result of buying the cards will not keep the yard in order. Any decision you make that doesn't support the mission or aid in the completion of your objective is an unwise use of your assets and resources. We would say that it is 'uneconomical' because it is not 'judicious.' You see, you cannot make wise decisions if you don't know what your mission is. This is the same for individuals, families, companies, and governments. When you begin to lose sight of your mission, your economy will begin to fail and eventually go bust. Do you understand this?"

"I think I do."

"Okay then. Do you remember that I told you that economies were based more upon human desire than upon money? Are you beginning to see what I meant by that?"

"Yes, Dad. It seems to me that the mission changes from person to person because of what each person might want. A guy may spend his money on things that I might think are stupid, but he is just following his own desires."

My father smiled a bit and continued, "You're getting so close to really understanding some of the basic principles of economics, but you're not quite there yet. What you should begin to see is that the mission determines the economy. Do you see that?"

"Yeah, Dad, I get that."

"Very good. Now, when controlling or managing an economy, there are a few things to consider. The first is the ultimate purpose for controlling an economy; it is to maintain as much of your wealth and resources, and to minimize, as much as you can, any debts you may produce while fulfilling the mission. If we go back to the term 'judicious use,' we are actually saying an 'efficient use.' The wise decision is aimed at increasing the efficiency of any operation. The end result of efficiency is either to increase the income or reduce the expenses. It comes down to a very simple mathematical equation. Do you understand this idea?"

The basic simplicity of economics was becoming clear to me at this point. Later in life, my father would explain to me how economists created huge misunderstandings in their field to confuse people. They developed a specific nomenclature and devised difficult terms and complicated mathematical models to obscure the obvious, common sense approach to this essential aspect of our lives.

Dad continued, "So, let's talk mathematics. Here is the simple term I want you to remember. Just think of the equal sign. On the left side of the equal sign, place your income and on the other, your outgoing expenses. If your income is equal to your expenses, you are not creating wealth. If your income is more than your expenses, you are creating wealth. You got that?"

"Yeah, that's simple."

"Okay. Now, what happens if your income is less than your expenses?"

"If it's less, than I'm losing everything."

"You've got it. Not only are you not getting wealthy, you are going into a hole and losing your income before you've even earned it. Always remember, *you should never spend more than you earn.* To be secure in life doesn't necessarily mean you have to make a lot of money; it really means having little to no debts to pay because this puts in jeopardy everything you have put together."

I pondered a few things as my father sipped some of

his coffee. What came to mind was how some people could buy more expensive things than others even though they seemed to be in similar circumstances. I posed this question to him and he responded.

"Well, Tommy, there are many things you have to consider. Some people may have the same income as we do, but have less expenses. They may have one child or no children at all. They may have had a better start financially than we did. Maybe they inherited money from a relative or something. In any case, if they are not living beyond their means, they have wisely budgeted their money so that they have enough wealth to purchase luxuries with their excess money."

"Excess money?"

"Yes. Some people have expenses much less than their income and this leaves them with disposable income that they can use to buy luxury items. They can take this money and splurge, or they can save it or invest it and put it to work for them."

"Dad, how can money work?"

"Tommy, remember how we just talked about resources? Money is as much a resource as anything else. It is an asset that can be used to improve efficiency and productivity. If a person wants to invest his money in a company that promises to return it to him with interest, his money will earn him more money. If I give you ten dollars for a project that will earn you fifty dollars, you can then give me fifteen back and have thirty-five in your pocket. We both have increased our wealth. The money I gave you will have 'worked' for both of us."

I didn't know it at the time, but my father was describing capitalism to me without using the term. This would be the subject of another, future conversation – one which would totally shatter the lies of my social studies teachers. In the meantime, we were interrupted and my father cut short the lesson. I stuffed my belongings into my pockets and went off to find my buddies, who were going to the woods to catch some turtles.

CHAPTER 15

THE WATERS OF GRAVELLY RUN

Passing from the open, mid-day sunlight into the tree line, I felt an immediate drop in the temperature from the shade produced by the canopy of the woods. The trail I was on was an old deer path that led directly to the creek some 250 yards from the trailhead. As I trotted my way down the grade to the meeting place, I thought about the lesson my father had just given me about economics. One of the things he said in passing kept running through my mind: economics applies to all life forms. When I arrived at the creek, my friends were nowhere to be found. I saw no signs of fresh tracks and heard no noises other than the birds and the sound of flowing water. I decided to take my sneakers and socks off and sit on a downed ash tree that bridged the creek. My dangling feet made small wakes in the moving water.

Gravelly Run, the actual name of the waters running between my feet, is a small creek at the bottom of a valley between the towns of Magnolia and Somerdale, New Jersey. Geographically, the valley is about a half a mile wide at its thinnest part and gradually widens to about a mile and a half as it runs west towards the town of Glendora. The run meanders about two miles towards a watery fork and merges with the Otter Brook to the North Branch of the Big Timber Creek just north of a place called Button Ball, off of Chews Landing Road. To the Lenni Lenape Tribe that inhabited the area, the creek was known as the *'Tetamekanchz,'* with the Chews Landing section being called the *'Arwames.'* During the time of the Revolutionary War, there was a skirmish there between the Continental Regulars and a British patrol. It was a place of awe for us kids and there were all sorts of legends about heavy weapons that the Continentals dumped into the creek to avoid confiscation by the British.

As I sat there, I heard some noise among the branches of a great oak, some fifteen yards away up the slope above the creek. I watched as three grey squirrels chased each other around the branches. This particular oak was very well-known to the kids that frequented the valley. From its branches, one of us fell and broke his collar bone. The tree had to be almost a thousand years old and it took three of us holding hands to circle the trunk's circumference. There were very few majestic, ancient trees among the other oaks, maples, black walnuts, and ashes that were the bulk of the species making up our small corner of the woodland. By the look of them, very few were more than 200 or 300 years old, especially those at the bottom of the valley on the south side of the creek. During the summer months, this single oak tree blocked more than a quarter of an acre of sunlight under its huge umbrella of foliage. The ground beneath was completely bare of any other trees or saplings, although some small shrubs grew in the indirect rays of the sun at the outermost extent of its branches. My eyes returned to the waters flowing below me. As I glanced at the downed ash tree upon which I sat, I suddenly realized that its roots were on the north bank of the creek. I then gazed downstream and saw that, without exception, every tree on the north bank, all of which were rooted within ten feet of the run, was leaning over the flowing water, while on the south bank all of the trees were erect, shooting straight up into the air. I pictured in my head all of the downed trees along the course of the creek, which I knew well, and realized that, without exception, all had fallen from north towards the south. Suddenly, a vision came to me and showed me what this place must have looked like hundreds of years before. The key to understanding this was that great old oak. It had stood for a thousand years in its place about twenty feet above the level of the present day run of water. In fact, all of the older trees were at or above that level, even on the opposite slope of the valley. This told me that it sprouted within ten feet of the water's edge on the north bank all of those many years ago and, because all of the trees south of the creek on the flood plain were much younger, there must have been a small lake here, possibly from a beaver dam downstream. The floor of the valley was then gradually populated with trees after the water level had dropped some three hundred years before, since the oldest trees there were about that age. I sat there in wonder. I had never looked at the woods in this way, nor had I ever seen it as more than a collection of trees. My thoughts were interrupted again by those grey squirrels. They seemed to be at an all-out state of war.

Anyone unfamiliar with nature looking at those three squirrels would have thought they were playing, but I knew better: they were actually trying to lay claim to the tree. As I looked at that oak, something came over me and I felt slightly stunned. It was a sense of acute clarity that I had never experienced before. If I had known the word at the time, I would have called it an epiphany. My father's words came back to my mind and echoed in my head, "economics applies to all life forms…" The sun, the creek, the fallen ash, the woods, the oak, the squirrels, the clearing under the oak, they all seemed to become one. The interplay between these seemingly disparate things solidified in my mind.

I recalled watching the squirrels and chipmunks collecting acorns in the fall. The squirrel that controlled the tree controlled the resources for food and nesting rights among the branches; the chipmunk who controlled the ground below did the same. That tree had to produce tens of thousands of acorns every season for at least a thousand years, and yet there were no other oaks growing within a radius of at least two hundred feet of its trunk. If there were no oaks in the area where the acorns had fallen from the branches, there had to be a reason. There also had to be a reason that there were other oaks growing outside the shadow of its leafy umbrella. I began to look around and count the other oaks, regardless of their ages, and noticed there were many of them, each at a good distance from the others. I tried to envision eliminating all the other species of trees to imagine what the woods would look like if it were only made up of oaks and was astonished at the picture. It appeared that each oak tree was the distance of the radii of its and the next tree's branches. Looking at the other dominant species of tree, I observed that they were straight and very few had lower branches. They gave me the impression that they shot up to punch a hole in the canopy. It became crystal clear that all of the species were in competition with each other and with their own kind. It also became obvious to me that that great oak, by far the oldest of its kind by at least 600 to 700 years, was the progenitor of all of the oaks in the valley. Considering only the oaks, they were inseparable from the squirrels and chipmunks. These were the carriers of the acorns beyond the umbrella of the tree that produced them. These animals hide the acorns as a future food source in the winter. They don't keep maps and are not perfect in their recall of just where they hide their food; some are forgotten. The animal that hides the acorns may even die, leaving the hidden oak nut to follow its destiny. It is their fallibility that gives the acorn a chance to sprout and flourish outside of its parent's dominion. I came to the conclusion that this species of tree and those two species of animal were tied together through a thousand generations. My father's economic lesson was beginning to make more and more sense to me. Though I felt illuminated, I still had some questions. I tied the shoelaces of my sneakers together, stuffed the socks inside one of them and threw them over my shoulder. I stood up and walked down the trunk to the bank and jumped down. When my feet hit the dirt, I felt a jolt of excitement in my chest and ran like the wind up the grade to the tree line toward home.

When I arrived at the back door of our home, I took the garden hose and washed off my feet before going inside. I quickly put on my socks and sneakers, but left them untied, and ran inside to look for my father. I found him in the basement at his electronics workbench, one of his hobbies. His bench was filled with all sorts of electronic equipment and had a well-organized drawer system of various components.

"What are you making, Dad?"

"An audio amplifier from a schematic that Henk Groot gave me…"

I was able to get my father's attention and explained to him in detail what I had observed. He listened intently without interruption. When I had finished, he smiled.

"Tommy, I have a question for you. I want you to think about what you've just told me. Do you remember sitting on the tree?"

"Yeah."

"When that thought comes to your mind, do you see yourself sitting on the tree, or do you see what your eyes saw?"

I paused a moment and responded, "I see myself sitting on the tree."

My father smiled again and said, "That's what I thought. You were able to look past the trees and see the forest. Your observations are pretty good, for a kid your age. Do you want to talk about what it all means?"

"Well, I was thinking about what you said about economics. You said that it applies to all life forms. I think I got this from watching the squirrels on the oak."

"Yes, that's one part of a pretty complicated interplay between everything in the woods. You know, when you and your brother were too young to leave the yard, I took a long walk in the woods down there. I knew that, one day, you two would eventually be old enough to explore it and I wanted to see for myself if there were any dangers to avoid. It seemed peaceful enough to allow you to go there without any reservations. I do know the oak that you are talking about. It's the one with all of the initials carved in it."

"Yeah, the one that Mark fell from and broke his collar bone."

"Mark is a dumb kid! Anyway, remember we talked about economies being based upon a mission and that the mission is founded upon pursuing an individual self-interest?"

"Yeah."

"Can you tell me what the self-interest of an oak tree is?"

I never really thought about a tree's self-interests. In fact, I didn't think that trees could think about such things and yet they are alive. After a moment, I looked at my father and said, "I guess they want to live, just like any other living thing."

"Okay, let's start there. Everything in the woods, whether it be an animal or a tree, wants to survive. The flora, which is the general term for all green plants, may not have a brain or a nervous system or be capable of rational thought, yet it still wants to survive. This is its primary mission. Now, what does survival mean to a tree?"

"I've got to think about that, Dad. It has to have sunlight and water..."

"Yes, and what else? How about the proper soil?"

"Yeah."

"Okay, so what we are talking about is the survival of the individual tree. We don't have to necessarily go into the chemical processes of green trees, let's just say that for a tree to survive, the energy source is sunlight. It drives all of the plant's activities. Now, knowing this, can we not identify the *currency* of the woods as sunlight?"

"I'd say so. I already knew that."

"I'm sure you did. From what you just told me though, what you didn't realize was what a tree will do to get the maximum amount of sunlight. The trees in the forest are all competing with each other for the sunlight that drives them and the water and minerals in the soil that sustain them. The oak will spread out its limbs, pushing other trees aside and, by doing so, will stop even its own offspring from growing in its shade and competing with it in the future. They will lean out over the creek for the open space to seek more sunlight and risk being uprooted by the flow of water eroding the bank or by windstorms. These actions are to survive as an individual, but what about surviving as a species? They have to develop strategies to get their acorns to an area that provides the proper conditions to sprout and grow with less competition from other trees and oaks. By giving an incentive of a storable food source to the squirrel and the chipmunk, they also must produce acorns in large amounts with the hope that maybe one in thousands will become a tree..."

"Yeah, Dad, that's exactly what I was thinking. It was like I was seeing it all happening in my mind. I also thought about some other things, like what would happen if the squirrels and chipmunks disappeared..."

"Tell me what you thought."

"Well, I was thinking that the oaks live a really long time, but the animals don't. The trees told me it took centuries to fill up the woods, and yet squirrels and chipmunks can only live a few years. There is another animal I know that also eats acorns, the blue jay. I was thinking that blue jays don't store food."

"And?"

"That means that the only way for an acorn to become a tree is if the jaybird drops it when he's flying around. I was wondering how many blue jays it would take to replace the number of acorns a squirrel would take and then lose to get new oak trees..."

"That's a good question. It seems that the blue jay is a

less efficient method of oak nut dispersal. There is another thing that you just glossed over that needs more thought, though."

"What's that?"

"Time! The trees live in one progression of time and the squirrels and chipmunks in another. To the animals, the oak is immortal and yet they would all seem to be linked together for their mutual survival. The oak has all the time in the world to reproduce, but the animals don't. Yet, the squirrel that misplaces the acorn today may be aiding the survival of his descendants a thousand years from now."

"That's what I was thinking! I thought to myself that was how that giant oak started out."

"Okay, now let's think in terms of economics. Do you remember our discussion?"

"Yeah."

"What is the oak tree in the grand scheme of things?"

"Well, I think that, to the animals, it is a resource. I was thinking that a lot of animals can eat its acorns, not just squirrels, chipmunks, and blue jays. Some animals build nests in its branches, too."

"Would you then say that the oak is providing a product and a service?"

"Yes."

"And, how is it paid for these?"

"I don't think it is paid, like with money. I think the animals trade the service of spreading around acorns for the oak and the tree exchanges it with food."

"That makes sense. So, what would the squirrel be to

the oak?"

"The squirrel is also a resource for the oak tree."

"You're right. There is an implied contract between the two species because, for all its greatness, the oak lacks the one thing that the squirrel has – legs. The squirrel offers the oak its mobility and the oak offers the squirrel its stability. The agreement is generational and mutually beneficial. It is a voluntary accord from which the entire woods benefit and, as you've already noticed, the relationship with the squirrel is the most efficient use of the oak's resources. There is the economy in action. Remember the definition?"

"Yeah, the judicious use of resources."

"Exactly. Among all of the animals, the most efficient way to spread around the acorns is by squirrel. And in reverse, it is in the individual squirrel's interest to dominate the oak. I believe that if you looked closely at all of the other species of trees in the woods, you'd find similar accords and similar strategies of voluntary relationships with other animals or insects."

"The other thing that I noticed was that the woods are not one solid block; there are three layers of the woods."

"What do you mean?"

"Well, there is the water layer, the ground layer, and the tree layer…"

"Oh, you mean there are three *strata*."

"Yeah, strata. All of the animals I thought of live in their own place. Some in or near the water, some on the ground, and some in the trees. Sometimes, they can move from one to another, like the squirrels, chipmunks, and birds. Some can't, like a box turtle can't climb a tree. But there's another thing, too. Some animals will do the same thing at night that other animals do during the day. It's like the woods are not only divided into those strata, but also into day and night. That makes six strata!"

"It does get pretty complicated, doesn't it? You know, Tommy, there is a science that studies the interrelationships of these things. It's called ecology. What do you think this word means?"

I had heard the word before, but only in school. It never dawned on me that the root word was the same as the root word of 'economy.' Here, my father went on to describe another concept of economics.

"The word 'ecology' also comes from the Greek word '*oikos*,' but instead of '*nemein*,' the word '*logos*' is used. This word meant 'speaking of' originally in Greek, but today we take it to mean 'the study of.'"

"So, it means 'the study of our home?'"

"Yes, that's right! And, there is no mystery that both words are linked by a common root. All wealth, in one way or another, comes from nature. If someone really wants to study a free economy in action, one not interfered with by external forces, like a government, nature is the way to do it."

I left this discussion with my head spinning with all of the possibilities of interrelationships of life down by the Gravelly Run. This day would have more of an effect upon me than I could have known then. It would eventually direct my interests into the biological sciences and then into healthcare as an adult. I often reflect upon how different my life would have been had my friends been waiting there by the fallen ash tree and I was not left to my thoughts and observations on that summer day

UNALIENABLE

when I was nine.

CHAPTER 16

THE LONGHORN BATTALION

Every once in a while, my father would relate some interesting stories about his war years. He never went into details of the battles themselves, other than to tell where he received his wounds. As was mentioned earlier, when he returned to Hawaii from Philadelphia after his father had died, he was re-assigned to the 39th Seabees. This battalion was organized in Texas and he found himself with only two or three other northerners. One of his mates was from Massachusetts and was the son of an Italian immigrant named Zappazutto. He was a fisherman by trade and the years of working on those rigs gave him a bodybuilder's physique. He was well over six feet tall and, with one arm, could pick up a man and lift him over a mess table. My father was much smaller than he, and Zap, as my father called him, often came to my father's defense even though he didn't really need it. I'm pretty sure that my father and Zap were the only two of Italian descent in the 39th and they were subject to many verbal attacks, but it never got physical. Zap was just too damned big to mess with and my father was a flyweight boxing champion until a Philippino decked him in a match. Interestingly, the guys made more jokes about them being northerners rather than being the sons of Italian immigrants. One joke my father recalled was indirectly aimed at him while they were all bunked down one night on Midway Island. One of his mates blurted out, "I were fifteen 'fo' I found out 'damned Yankee' was two words!" This got a cackling laugh out of the rest of the men that heard it. My dad's response to him was, "And that was two years before you got your first pair of shoes!" These light-hearted jabs were never taken seriously and after the first battle alongside the 2nd Marines, they all had a healthy respect for one another.

There was another Seabee battalion that was formed in Texas. Until sometime in 1943, both of these groups referred to themselves as the Lone Star Battalion and, every time they met, they got into knock-down, drag out fights over who had the rights to the name. It became so much of a problem early on that Admiral Chester Nimitz, who was also a Texan, had to step in and calm the situation down. It was he who gave the name Longhorn Battalion to the 39th. He convinced the men by explaining that the longhorn cattle were the life's blood of Texas and were a good mascot because 'they had two long horns and a lot of bull in between!' When my father got to the battalion, the argument, which really meant nothing to him personally, was already settled.

UNALIENABLE

When one thinks of the war in the Pacific, the subject of economy doesn't frequently come to mind. However, my father explained to me that there was a booming economy among the men on those islands and the Seabees were in the middle of it all.

When the 39th got to Midway Island, they saw their first opportunity to make some deals with souvenirs. Several of the men began buying and trading everything that they believed could turn a profit. As they started island-hopping from Midway to Kwajalein and Eniwetok, they created side businesses manufacturing and selling goods and services to the GIs, Marines, and swabbies.

On Saipan, a few of my father's mates found an old steam engine. They cannibalized it and took the boiler to use for heating up water for showers. This service became the centerpiece for an entire system of economics. The GIs and Marines traded battlefield souvenirs for hot showers. Some of the souvenirs were then swapped with the swabbies for ice cream powder pilfered from their ship's messes. The Seabees would then make ice cream in their messes for the Marines or GIs to buy or trade for other souvenirs. Aside from the obvious battlefield souvenirs, such as flags, bayonets, pistols, swords and knives, among the most looked-for finds were Japanese searchlights. The reflectors were lined with pure silver. The Seabees took this silver, melted it down, and made rings in their machine shops. One searchlight reflector could produce more than ten rings. Some of the Seabees would spend their off-duty time collecting specific types of seashells, which they would then polish to a high sheen, turning them into "cat's eyes" to be set into the rings. The asking price for these rings was about $50.00.

My father told me that, on one of his outings while off-duty, he fell into a hidden bunker while moving inland from Tanapag Harbor. Inside, he found a small, wooden crate filled with Nambu Type 14 pistols. He brought these pistols back to the Seabee base, sold some and traded others for credit to other suppliers of services in the mess. He kept one for himself. These pistols were the type of good which were given to officers to turn a blind eye, allowing the Seabees to continue their entrepreneurial activities.

For the GIs and Marines picking up battlefield souvenirs, there was a risk. The Japanese would often booby-trap objects and the unskilled collector could be severely wounded or killed by tampering with them. The value placed upon items brought in from the field took this risk into consideration.

The machinist mates in the shops also produced personalized items for the Marines and GIs, such as raider knives, Bowie knives, and weapon modifications. The raider knives were especially interesting in that they had a long, slender blade and brass knuckles for a handle. In hand-to-hand combat, one could punch and slash in one motion and return and jab in the rebound. My father carried such a knife himself.

By war's end, my dad had a decent collection of battlefield souvenirs he wanted to bring home. They filled a good-sized, canvas sea bag. During transport back to Hawaii, all of the Seabees kept a close eye on their belongings for fear that some swabby would steal them. My dad's company spent most of their time on deck, sitting around, smoking, reading, and playing cards to break up the boredom, keeping their belongings next to them. At one point, a Navy Lieutenant, Junior Grade approached my father and asked him what he had in the bag. My father respectfully explained to him that it was none of his business. The officer ordered my father to remove the lock so he could inspect the contents. My father refused. The officer then told my father that there were regulations against transporting contraband and threatened him with the brig and possibly a Captain's Mast offence. By this time, most of his mates in earshot were following the discussion. My father then picked up the bag, walked to the gunwale, and heaved it overboard. Returning to where he was seated on the deck, he told the officer, "You want to inspect the bag? Go take a swim for it."

My father was brought before the Captain of the ship for his insubordination. When the situation was explained to him by the Lieutenant, the Captain told the Lieutenant that he was lucky that he wasn't thrown overboard instead of the bag and ordered my father to return to his mates on deck. My father came home with no souvenirs from his seventeen battles and three major wounds, but his sacrifice enabled the rest of his company to return unmolested by Naval officers attempting to steal Seabee goods. This was my father's way of telling me that it was preferable to chuck all of his stuff overboard into the depths of the Pacific by his own choice, rather than be coerced into handing it over to someone who didn't earn or deserve it through their own efforts or sacrifices.

Years later, our home was burgled and the thieves stole his battle ribbons and medals, including his Purple Hearts. He told me that if someone would have been kind enough to steal his malaria and jungle-rot, he would have had nothing left to remind him of the war, but he had forgotten one souvenir that appeared by chance before his death.

While I was in Italy, my father called and described to me some strange signs and symptoms he was experiencing. I suggested that he make an appointment with my friend, Dr. Frank Pettinelli, Jr. When the results of the exams came back, Frank called me and told me to come home; he suspected bladder cancer. I returned in time to go over the imaging and make introductions with a fine urologist, Dr. Kenneth Brownstein at Thomas Jefferson University Hospital in Philly. During the car ride home from the Imaging Center at Kennedy Hospital, I opened up my father's MRI envelope and reviewed the films. In the lower, right quadrant of the abdomen, there was a starburst artifact sprayed across the image. Had the radiologist known that there was a piece of metal there, he would not have done the MRI. When I told my dad that what I was seeing seemed to be a jagged chunk of metal lodged into his abdomen just above his ileocecal valve, he replied that it was a piece of shrapnel from a

Japanese bomb. Evidently, when he was wounded, the surgeon just sutured him up without removing the metal.

"I've been living on borrowed time since I was nineteen. They had three chances to kill me then and I beat them," he told me.

This souvenir he would take with him to his grave.

CHAPTER 17

FRIEDMAN'S FOUR WAYS OF SPENDING MONEY

My father was a great admirer of Dr. Milton Friedman. He also admired many other economists, from Adam Smith and onward to Carl Menger, Ludwig von Mises, Friedrich von Hayek, Murray Rothbard, Thomas Sowell, and many others too numerable to mention here. His views on economics merged concepts from both The Austrian and The Chicago Schools of Economics. He fused these approaches to economic interpretation with theoretical business management models to validate what was observed and studied by people like Henri Fayol and Frederick Taylor. He also included the psychological perspectives on human motivations by Abraham Maslow. He viewed economics from the perspective of voluntary interactions between people, as though they were following the Natural Laws that were the underpinning of all free exchanges.

He was not a fan of Karl Marx nor of John Maynard Keynes.

One day, when I was nearing eighteen, I came home to find my father sitting at the kitchen table. Though he had a cup of coffee in front of him, he uncharacteristically had no reading material in his hands. He seemed pensive, but I sensed an air of disgust. My father never showed his emotions openly, but my brothers and I could always tell what his moods were by his body language.

We greeted each other as I came into the room and went to the sink to wash my hands. I looked at him and asked him what was on his mind.

He responded, "You remember when you were a kid and I gave you an allowance to do chores around the house and yard work? I had two reasons for doing this: one was to motivate you to contribute to maintaining the household, but the other was to teach you the meaning of work and the value of both your time and the money you earned. You understood that quickly. I remember how you saved your money for that walkie-talkie and how you disciplined yourself to put away what you could. You learned on your own how to budget."

"I remember. I also remember that you matched what I had saved so that I could get the walkie-talkie before Christmas."

"I matched your savings as a reward because I understood that you already learned the lessons I was trying to teach you."

"Is this what you were thinking about before I came in?"

"No. I was reflecting upon something I heard Dr. Friedman say about spending money and how true it is."

"Why is that?"

"Well, today I had a short discussion with the President of the college and he was a bit upset with me. You know that I received a federal grant to research and compile the educational system I'm designing, right?"

"Yeah?"

"I projected it to take about three years to do, for which the federal government granted me the monies to be disbursed in three yearly installments. Last week, my first fiscal year for the project ended and I found that there was an excess of monies. In other words, we came in under budget."

"That's a good thing, isn't it?"

"I think so. So, what I did was return the excess money to the federal department that gave me the grant with a revised budget for next year that was less than the first, especially considering that all of the office equipment and major supply expenses were already paid for. I was called to the President's office this morning and sat through a cordial lecture on how to be corrupt! I felt like a kid being called to the principal's office to be chastised!"

"What?"

My father went on to describe his meeting with the President who, in no uncertain terms, told him that he "didn't know how to play the game," that he should have spent the excess monies on anything he could have used to justify it, and increased the projected budget for the next year by at least 20%!

"When I realized what he was saying, and the tone with which he said it, I gave him a stern lecture of my own. I reminded him that the government had entrusted *me* with the People's money for this project and that I had complete oversight. I also told him that I know precisely how the game is played, I'm just not playing it and if we come in under budget for this year, the overage will again be returned and the third year's budget will also be revised downward. There was no way he, or anyone else, was going to get me to steal the People's money and taint the system I was trying to create."

"What did he say?"

"What *could* he say? He was telling me to steal grant money! I told him that the conversation never took place and that he called me to his office for a cup of tea. I then excused myself and left."

Aside from this questionable morality, the President was not much of a visionary either. I remember that my father, having come to the college from RCA, where he had created a system for teaching the COBOL and FORTRAN computer languages, wrote a proposal to add a curriculum for computer sciences to the college offerings early in the 1970s. This was smirked at by this same man, who proclaimed to my father, "Computers are a passing fad, Mario!" It wasn't very long afterwards that he had to eat his words and my father dusted off his proposal and re-submitted it for consideration to the Board of Directors. It was approved, of course.

"Dad, you said you were thinking about something Dr.

Friedman said."

"Yes, that's right. This meeting reminded me of one of the four ways Milton Friedman said there were of spending money. It's a brilliant observation and explains why anything involving a government costs much more than any private sector spending for similar projects."

"Well, what did he say?"

"First, I'm only talking about the ways to spend money and not whether there is a benefit to society; we'll leave that argument out of it. The first is the way I taught you when you were a kid – you can spend your own money on yourself. Generally, you are very cautious and want to get the maximum return for the money that you've earned through your own labor. You know what the value of that money is because you know what it took to earn it. When you want a service or a product, you have to decide whether the money in your pocket is less desirable to you than what you want. Does it make sense that this is the most efficient way for you to spend money?"

"Yes."

"The second way is for you to spend your money on someone else. Let's say you want to buy a gift for your mom's birthday. You're still spending your money, but for your mom's benefit. Three things come into play here: the value you place on your mother's enjoyment, the value you place on your money, and the value you place on the gift. You still want the maximum value for your money, but would be willing to spend a bit more because the object you're buying also has the emotional factor of your mother's reaction added to it. You see, the gift's value in and of itself is added to the value you perceive in your mom's reaction."

"That makes sense to me."

"The third way is where you are spending someone else's money on yourself. Let's say you work for a company that gives you an open expense account for meals, travel, and lodging. You can use it to eat, say, at either a fast-food place or a five-star restaurant. You will be less cautious on how you spend that money than if it were your own, but you will still be mindful that you have to answer to someone to justify the expense. You would naturally place more value on your own pleasure or satisfaction and spend more than is necessary. This is a less efficient way to spend money because the value of what you're getting is less dependent upon the amount of what you're spending on it. Businesses often use this as a meter of the loyalty of the employee. Someone in accounting will be reviewing the expenses at some point."

"Can't a business write those expenses off on their taxes?"

"Yes, but how a person respects the money of their employer often reflects upon how they would respect other aspects of the company's operations and property. It can also be a measure of how much trust the employer can reasonably place upon the future actions of the employee."

"That happened to me, once. Mr. Bunt sent me up to north Jersey for an auto part that he needed faster than it could be delivered. He gave me the money to pay for the part but also $20.00 for tolls, gas, and food. I went up and back but didn't stop to eat and gave him the change when I got back to the station. He gave the money right back to me and told me to get something to eat."

"Can I ask you why you gave him the rest back?"

"Well, I was on the clock the whole time. I normally punch out for a half-hour for lunch and buy it myself. I didn't see any reason for him to buy me lunch. To my mind, the money I gave him back wasn't mine. It was his."

"I see..."

"That's three, Dad. You said there were four."

"Yes. The fourth way is when you spend someone else's money for the benefit of yet another person. This is the least efficient and most wasteful way of spending. The money is not yours so there is no regard for its worth. Since it is being spent on something for someone else, you don't care about the price nor if that price is reasonable. This is how the government spends the People's money. Those in government see an endless supply of it and spend like there is no tomorrow on projects the private sector most often would never even dream of getting involved with. Can you see how a hammer that I can buy for $5.00 privately could wind up costing $50.00 when the Pentagon buys it? There is a general rule that anything done by a government will cost at least five times what it would have cost in the private sector and it will take at least five times the time to complete. Another aspect of this is that the government, having the money available, will look everywhere for something to spend it on and for no good reason other than to push a political end that favors individuals at the expense of the rest of us – "bridges to nowhere" comes to mind. Bad management is another factor. In the private sector, badly run companies risk going bankrupt and their management gets the boot; anything run by the government just asks for more appropriations and those who are badly managing the organizations remain where they are to worsen everything still further. These are all the result of this fourth way of spending money."

He continued showing example after example of how government involvement in the mismanagement of the People's money is so common that it is hardly ever questioned and is even accepted as a normal function of government. My father went on to say that it was not just merely a question of how the People's money is spent badly, but how it is spent unwisely. Often, the government will spend money in ways that conflict with common sense.

He listed all of the government agencies that cost the taxpayers billions of dollars by directly subsidizing some private sector industries. He explained that those same agencies write up costly regulations that drive out industry and deter foreign companies from competing in our markets.

His brief encounter with the president of his college illustrated precisely what is wrong with government spending. Whenever a government agency talks about "oversight", what we should hear is "shell game" with the "pea" being inefficiency, waste, and outright theft.

CHAPTER 18

Why Things Go Bust

It was an afternoon sometime in December of 1974. I was preparing for the final exams in my first semester at college, and I went downstairs to get a cup of coffee. I found my father sitting at the kitchen table. He was reading an old, yellowed copy of *The Road to Serfdom* by Friedrich Hayek. The book looked like he had read it before and many of the pages were dog-eared. He prized this book and considered it one of the most insightful ever written on the analysis of the threat of tyranny predicated by government control of economics through central planning.

In the beginning of September of that same year, I had returned from a summer-long trip to Chile, where I had seen first-hand the devastating results of Marxism applied to an otherwise productive society. From what I saw, it was nothing to be wished for.

He said to me, "You know, every time I read this book,

I find something new to reflect upon. You've seen with your own eyes in Chile what leftist ideology causes and you've interpreted it correctly. If you were to read this book, you'd realize that Hayek predicted it back in the 1940s."

"It makes you wonder why all of the insanity is constantly repeated! I mean, if Germany and Italy came crashing down, why would Chile have started on that road to begin with?"

"It's either from historical and economic ignorance or propaganda or both! Most of the people that I know who believe in the Marxist claptrap act as if there was no history before they were born. Tommy, the war wasn't even over yet and the academics in Britain and the U.S., along with the Democrat party, were already distancing themselves from their Nazi and Fascist brothers. They just absolutely would not admit to the truth and give up on their dogma. They couldn't convince people that there was anything good that came out of those regimes so they immediately started spreading the lie that these were a *capitalist* reaction to socialism. Imagine that! Hayek defied that view. He maintained rightly that Fascism and Nazism had shared, Marxist origins in central economic planning and the consolidation of the state over the individual. It was clearly obvious that when individualism is abolished, there will be an unavoidable loss of freedom, the establishment of a tyrannical dictator, and then serfdom. This is the primary difference between our way of life and the Marxist's way – we are convinced that our rights and freedoms are *unalienable* and they want to force upon the world their belief that we have no rights and are subservient to a governmental authority. If anything, Fascism and Nazism were the *socialist* reaction to the failure of Marxism to convince the working classes that their lives were not improving under free market capitalism. When the Depression hit, who do you think the socialists blamed? Of course - the greedy capitalists, the capitalist market, and capitalism itself. This was all a lie. Capitalist principles see money as a commodity resource in the market. It doesn't have anything to do with the central planners of central banks playing around with the money supply."

I sat down with my coffee and asked, "Why the renewed interest in Hayek?"

He smiled, "Maybe you didn't hear. Hayek just won the Nobel Prize in Economics!"

I hadn't heard since I was concentrating more on my studies than recent events.

My father continued, "I'm happy to see that Hayek has finally been recognized for his explanation of the business cycle. I'm reading this again because the prize validates the premise of the book."

"How is that?"

"Have you got a few minutes? There is a line of reasoning behind the explanation for 'why things go bust.'"

"Sure, go ahead..."

He began, "Okay. Well, during the 1800s, we had a series of economic crises starting from 1819 which had devastating effects. They occurred in cycles of about every twenty years all the way through to the beginning of the 1900s and each lasted, on average, between four and six years. The economists were at a loss to explain these 'panics', as they called them. They usually were triggered by the failure of a bank or crops or something that was seemingly trivial and rippled throughout the entire economy. Along comes Ludwig von Mises who writes what is probably the best book ever written on money as a market commodity called *The Theory of Money and Credit*. In this book, he touches on the role of money itself, through the concept of what is called the 'marginal utility of value' as the major cause of these panics, linking the emotional value that individuals place upon money to the concept of 'supply and demand,' leading to 'industrial fluctuations.' However, what Mises failed to realize was that it was a function of the supply of money in and of itself as a commodity and inflationary credit at artificially low interest rates that were the actual problems. The individual's subjective value placed upon money was only minimally involved."

"Dad, I don't know what you mean by 'marginal utility of value'…"

"Well, it really is a simple concept – the more you have of something, the less you value each additional unit. In other words, if you only have a hundred dollars, another hundred is a big deal. If you have a million dollars, a hundred more means little to you. You get the idea? This applies not just to money, but the subjective value of products and services too. Your first buggy whip may cost you $10 and be worth it to you. You would be less likely to purchase another at the same price because you already have one and you can't use two of them at the same time. To apply this idea to industrial fluctuations, suppose there is a product in great demand in the market. Several companies then go into production when the price of the product is high. As they compete and the price drops and the more the demand is satisfied, the less the product is desired and the unsold supply begins to rise. The price begins to drop even more and the companies producing the product begin to see a decline in the profitability of producing it. If they don't find another product to make, they go out of business. Someone watching this can see failure on the horizon if the company they work for is getting a larger and larger share of an ever-decreasing market. This is what they referred to as the 'average period of production.' You see what I mean?"

"Yes."

"Hayek recognized that Mises was onto something, but he realized that marginal utility of value fell a bit short of a reasonable explanation for the panics. He studied carefully the roles of capital, the money supply, credit and interest rates prior to the panics, and realized that these crises always followed widespread inflationary credit expansion and its communication over time, leading to a capital misallocation caused by the artificially low interest rates."

"I'm not sure I see how this works? How can interest rates lead to a misallocation of capital?"

"Here's where things get interesting. You first have to

know how banks operate and the criteria they use to set interest rates. When we were on a precious metal standard – that is, gold and silver - the money supply was relatively fixed. These metals were treated as any other commodity and their relative value was set by the market according to their supply. This was not really subject to inflation. However, the currency we have circulating in society is also accompanied by the total amount of credit given by lending agents. Credit, because it is a promise to pay, is inflationary if there is nothing backing that promise in hard currency. It works like this: let's say you deposit a hundred dollars in a bank for the promise of a 3% return in interest. The bank then lends that money out at 6% and you both share the return. If the bank has a policy to lend out only what it has in reserve, then everything works out fine. What happens if the bank makes one hundred-dollar loans to three people and only has your hundred on reserve? This represents four hundred dollars in circulation – the money you think you've got and the three hundred dollars that the others think they have access to. Can you see that this can have an effect on the overall purchasing power of these dollars? It isn't obvious with just this little example, but imagine that every bank is competing with each other in the same way throughout the entire economy?"

"It sounds like a giant Ponzi scheme, to me. So, you're saying that the banks were causing inflation by expanding credit."

"Yes, even when we didn't have the federal reserve system, the state-chartered banks collectively acted the same way. The house of cards is destined to collapse when you go to the bank and withdraw your money and the merchants who were paid by those three loan-holders with the bank's credit do the same. The bank can't cover the payments and shuts the doors. We would call this a 'bank run' because it spreads panic to all of the depositors. Now, this was the major reason that the Federal Reserve System used to justify its creation. Instead of creating laws forcing banks to have ethical lending practices, they came along with a scheme to plug the holes in the money supply on reserve in the bank. So, while the depositors and creditor merchants are banging on the front door, the Federal Reserve is coming in the back door with the money that should have been in the vault. In order for this scheme to work to their satisfaction, however, the Fed eventually had to drive out the hard currency and replace everything with their own IOUs – the Federal Reserve Notes that we call dollar bills today. So now, not only is credit subject to inflation, but so is the money supply in circulation. Now, rather than having the proper amount of hard currency on reserve for lending, the law only requires that banks have 10% on reserve for what they lend out. We refer to this as 'fractional reserve banking.' The Fed prides itself on having stopped the 'panics' and they did! They just re-named it a 'recession' or 'depression' and never referred to it as a panic, again."

"How clever! And what about the interest rates?"

"Here is the most interesting part of Hayek's observations. The people in industry have no idea how much credit the banks are issuing. They can only have an idea on the hard money supply. They trusted the banks to echo the amount of people's savings by the interest rates they were asking for loans. Now, listen carefully, because this was the brilliant observation that Hayek made. When you or I deposit money into the bank, we consider this an asset because it earns us interest. From the point of view of the bank, it is a liability! They can only make money if they lend it out – their money is considered an asset to them if it's on the street earning interest and not in their vault paying interest! Is the idea clear to you?"

"Yeah, I get that."

"Okay, now, under ideal conditions with ethical lending policies, when people are saving more and more money, the banks start to have a glut on the money in their vaults. They have to incentivize people to take out loans by reducing the interest rates, just to get it out of their vaults to reduce their liabilities. Industry looks at these reductions in interest rates and interprets this as people saving money. This tells them that this money will be available in the future for the purchase of new products. So, how do you think industry would respond?"

"Well, by planning to make different goods to sell and get a jump on the competition?"

"Very good! They take out loans at low interest for research and development of new products and the purchase of new capital for production with the hope that they can pay off these loans with future profits. They start to reallocate their resources from the production of things that people would otherwise buy today and go into the production of things that people will buy sometime in the future. Hayek realized that free market economics was essentially an information stream! Is the idea clear?"

"Yes, it is."

"Okay, now what do you think would happen if the banks artificially lower their interest rates in a way that doesn't faithfully reflect the amount of savings in their vault? Industry gets hoodwinked into believing there will be spendable money in the future. Of course, that will never materialize. Not only have they lost potential, present-day profits by reallocating their resources, but when the future arrives, there will be no money around to purchase their new products. There will be far fewer profits from which they can re-pay their loans and they eventually go bankrupt! Everything comes crashing down!"

"Having it explained like this, it seems a pretty simple idea."

"Hayek opened many eyes with this analysis. Many economists have thrown stones at him, but their interpretations led nowhere. Murray Rothbard wrote the definitive thesis on the Panic of 1819 and it completely verified Hayek's interpretation – even before the existence of a central bank here."

We spoke a little more on Hayek and his Austrian Theory of the Business Cycle and had a good laugh at those who said it was all really just about *greed*. My father pointed out that he has never known greed, or any other human emotion, to occur in twenty-year cycles. Socialists never seem to understand that private capitalism is an economic system and not a political one and that a governmental monopoly, like a central bank, can never have the wisdom, nor the proper information to determine a supply of money. Even if it did, it would never have the ability to use that information correctly.

CHAPTER 19

THE MINIMUM WAGE

In 1972, when I was not yet seventeen years old, I was able to get a job working at a gas station. The gas station was located on Kings Highway in Cherry Hill, New Jersey, which was one of the major roads in the town. The owner's name was Joseph Bunt and he had run his Gulf station for at least ten years at the same location. When I first started working for Joe, I was in high school and had relatively little skills to offer any new employer. This was nothing new to Mr. Bunt and he had, over the years of running his business, developed a method for training young people like me who were just entering the workforce.

Joe asked me if I had ever worked in a gas station before or if I had any experience with mechanics. I was honest with him and said that, although I had never worked before, I did have a good knowledge of mechanics that my Uncle Nick had taught me. My uncle was, at the time, the general manager of an SKF Bearing plant in Philadelphia. We had rebuilt a Simca from the ground up, which my cousin Nicky was to use for transportation to and from college. Additionally, I told him that I was good with motorcycles and small engines, and that I wasn't afraid to get my hands dirty. That seemed to be enough for Mr. Bunt to give me a chance.

We agreed that I would start out with a trial month to see how I settled in. He then asked me to come back in the next day. I agreed, thanked him, got on my motorcycle, and went home. It dawned on me that I hadn't even asked what he was going to pay me, which Joe later admitted was one of the things he liked about me.

The next day, I came to work and Joe introduced me to the other employees. One was Jim, who was working to put money aside for college. The other was a mechanic called John.

I was then given over to Jim, who took me into the station to give me a tour. The station was very clean and orderly. It had three garage bays, two of which had hydraulic lifts. In the back of the front office was a utility room that housed the compressed air tank, as well as the lockers for the employees' clothes and other belongings. There was also inventory storage. Jim showed me my locker and my uniforms and asked me to change so that we could go over my duties, which, I was surprised to see, were not very challenging.

That first day, I was handed a mop and bucket, industrial cleaners and detergents, and was told to clean the public lavatories. I did so. Apparently, I did so very quickly. When I reported back to Mr. Bunt that I was

UNALIENABLE

finished with the bathrooms, he asked me if I was sure because he was going to inspect them. I told him I was sure and that I would accompany him to see my work.

Mr. Bunt opened both bathroom doors and entered one after the other. When he came out, he praised me on the cleanliness of the rooms and the amount of time it took me to do them. Joe had a management theory which was quite refreshing; it was by objective. In other words, he didn't like "busy work" because, as he told me, "there is a big difference between action and motion." He would assign an objective and if you got it done to his satisfaction in half an hour, that was great. If you wanted to drag it out for three hours, that was okay too, as long as there were no other chores that had to be completed. However, everything had to be done by the end of the shift.

We returned to the front office, where Jim was reading a textbook, and Joe told him to get me familiar with the pump islands, the oil racks, and the procedures. Joe insisted that everyone who got gas had to have their windshields squeegeed clean and to be asked if they wanted their oil and fluids checked. If we recognized what looked like low tire pressure, we were told to check the pressure and fill the tire without asking. Joe knew how customers wanted to be treated and this was his way of giving more to them to keep their patronage. Additionally, it maintained the sale of motor oil, automatic transmission fluid, antifreeze, windshield wipers, tires, headlights and other light bulbs, which was good for the bottom line. We had a slew of regulars that knew us all by name and we frequently got tips, though Joe told us that wasn't the reason for us to provide the extra service.

Mr. Bunt knew his business and he knew it well. He knew not just the facets of his productivity, but also the financial aspects of the business.

For the next few days, I followed Jim around and learned the ropes of running a shift, though my chores remained relatively the same. I was taught how to calculate the number of gallons sold at each pump and to reconcile the cash and credit card receipts with the pump figures and other products sold. I was instructed to register the sales for inventory control and, since we were a Hertz Rental Car receiver, how to write up contracts and check in and properly clean incoming cars. I was learning quickly and taking on responsibilities and chores without being told. When I saw that something needed to be done, I did it without asking and my employer was pleased.

Within two weeks, I was running my own shift with all of the responsibilities that were implied. I was also responsible for the receipts at the end of that shift and all of the documentation for Joe to audit.

I was being paid the minimum wage, which, at that time, was $1.60 per hour. My schedule was from 3:00 pm to 9:00 pm five days a week and an eight-hour shift on Saturdays and Sunday mornings when school was in session. I was able to work a little more during school breaks and in the summers. In any case, I was working for about six months when Joe had a personal emergency and had to leave the shop early. He was working on a car and left his tools in disarray, which was very unlike him. When my shift ended, I punched the clock, locked up the station, and decided to clean and put his tools where they belonged. To my surprise, I heard someone knocking on the bay door. It was Joe, who had come by to pick up the receipts for deposit the next morning.

I opened the front office door and he asked me what I was still doing there. When I told him that I was cleaning and putting away his tools, he asked me who gave me permission to work that kind of overtime. I told him that I had punched out more than forty minutes before. He silently nodded his head a few times, raised his eyebrows and, after a pause, asked me if I was hungry. He took me to a nearby diner and I had a burger. We talked, for the first time, about what my plans were for the future and I told him I wanted to become a doctor. We each got to know one another a little better in that booth and I was surprised to see that he had kicked my hourly wage up to $1.75, on that Friday.

Over the course of the next two years, my skills improved and Joe taught me some mechanical work to help out in the garage. I was running the pump islands between brake jobs, tire mounting and balancing, hanging exhaust systems, packing bearings, doing oil changes and lube jobs, cutting disc brakes, and aligning frontends. I even got my friend Leon a job as an apprentice mechanic and all three bays were then active. Another employee came on board, Paul, who was in his late twenties and had a wife and son. He and his family had just moved to the area from the mid-west.

I was now earning $1.85 an hour. However, the price of gasoline and other petroleum products started to climb sharply because of the oil embargo. Our profit margin on sales was determined by the contracts we had for delivery from Gulf Oil as well as the octane rating of the gas. For Joe to be competitive, he had to look closely at those margins. Giving up a cent profit represented a good-sized loss on every gallon sold, but he figured he could stay ahead in volume and counter it with an increase in mechanical work. Prices went from about thirty-eight cents per gallon in 1973 to about fifty cents at the beginning of 1974. When the odd/even license plate rationing began, I had no time for any work inside the garage. The lines for gasoline made life practically impossible. Many stations around us ran out of gas within days of their deliveries. Ten-gallon limits were placed on the volume we could pump to individual cars. People argued. They cursed. They tried to cut in line and got in fistfights. Sometimes the police had to be called. Once, a woman tried to run over a man in the station lot. She missed him but hit the oil rack and ran over a few dozen cans of motor oil.

In January of 1974, the government ordered an increase in the minimum wage to $2.00 per hour. I didn't think much of it when it happened, but thought, "Hey, another 15 cents an hour is good." Without knowing it, I was about to learn a lesson from my father.

The day I was informed about the increase in the minimum wage, I returned home after my shift and sat down at the kitchen table to have dinner. My father, as usual, was reading a book while drinking a cup of coffee.

"Dad," I said, "Mr. Bunt told me that the minimum wage was increased to $2.00 an hour."

My father looked over his book and said, "I heard. Do you think that's a good thing?"

"Well, it's another fifteen cents an hour in my pocket," I responded.

UNALIENABLE

My father placed the open book pages down on the table. I knew that I was about to have something explained to me, but first he asked me to hand him the pad and pencil from the counter. He began asking me some general questions about the profit margins on gas, how we contracted for delivery, and how much we pumped per shift. I answered that we were now contracting the purchase only a month in advance. This meant that the retail sales price increases lagged behind the increases from the distributor. Our margins went from three and a half to five cents per gallon, depending upon the octane ratings. We were pumping between 1,000 to 1,500 gallons per shift. He wrote the figures down and did some simple calculations. He averaged out the numbers and said that if I only worked the pumps, I was generating between $40.00 to $60.00 in profits per shift. Dividing this figure over the average six hours that I worked per weekday, I would be generating $6.66 to $8.00 per hour for Mr. Bunt. On the weekends, it was even less because I was there for eight hours. Of course, this didn't take into account any reduction in the profit margin to undercut the competition. He reminded me that the contract prices were steadily increasing because of the fuel embargo and the fabricated shortages and that, though the retail price increase lagged a month behind the delivery of gas, the increasing wholesale prices for delivery had to be anticipated for the following month.

Next, my father asked me some questions about the personnel, their duties and their pay. I listed the employees by name and told him their functions. The mechanics, including my friend Leon, were averaging between three to four times what I was making. Jim was already preparing to leave for Perdue University in Indiana to study agronomy. He made about sixty cents an hour more than I did. None of these would be affected by the minimum wage increase, since they already made more than the government mandate. Paul and I made the same amount and were the only two directly affected. My father then inquired about Paul.

"Paul," I told him, "is about twenty-nine or thirty years old and has a wife and son. He moved here from somewhere in the mid-west about a year ago."

My father nodded and said, "Okay, you'd better prepare yourself to be out of a job in about two to three months…"

I said nothing but looked at him in surprise. He went on to give me the reasons for his statement and I received my first real lesson on the consequences of government mandates meant to fix wages above their real market value.

He told me that Mr. Bunt was a businessman. When he formed his company, his purpose was to create wealth for himself and his family and not to provide jobs for people. It was Joe who invested his time and money into the start-up and running of his business. It was Joe who had sacrificed, took on financial risk, and met his overhead in the lean years of operation. It was Joe who hired people without skills like me and trained them to improve their worth in the market place, increasing their earning capacity. As Joe's wealth increased, so did that of the people he employed. Everyone benefitted by Joe's activities. Unfortunately, Mr. Bunt was now being pushed against the wall by outside forces that were, essentially, placing a strain on his income. It was not simply the fifteen cents an hour increase that he had to pay me; it was also the increase in his overhead for utilities, inventory, auto parts, cleaning services for the uniforms, shop rags and all other outside services and products that the minimum wage would transmit to his operating costs from outside sources.

My father reminded me how Mr. Bunt had treated me with fairness. He saw my devotion and dedication to his business and rewarded me with training and an increasing paycheck that reflected my value to his company based upon that training. To my father, this meant that Mr. Bunt was a moral man and, given the choice between me and a married man with a child to support, Joe would be obligated to choose Paul over me. My father told me it would not be personal, but Joe was not there to run a charity and the way things were going, that mandated increase in my wages would force him to lay me off.

In March of 1974, Joe pulled me aside to talk to him in private. His eyes welled up as he told me he had to let me go. He started to explain the reasons why and I told him I already knew and that I had known from the time of the minimum wage increase. That Friday I received my last paycheck from Bunt's Gulf Station.

Looking clearly at my experience, I was able to enter into the workforce with relatively few skills. Yes, I was low-paid in the beginning, but I gradually increased my skill set as well as my value to the company and, as I did so, I was being paid progressively more. What my father pointed out to me was that minimum wage laws lose workers their jobs and prevent other people from entering the workforce at a wage appropriate to what their limited skill set could provide to the productivity and the profitability of a company. It dashes their possibility to get the skills which would earn them more in the future. There are other effects of these laws.

In most cases of services or product sales, business owners must pass on these increases to the consumer, meaning that people will have to pay more in order for these companies to just maintain their pre-mandate profit levels. Customers will notice this effect across the entire spectrum of the economy and along all of the orders of production. If businesses cannot compete, they will close their doors, sending their entire workforce to the unemployment lines. Tax revenues will be reduced in the venues where they once operated and resources will be lost or stagnated.

Additionally, and more socially important, minimum wage laws harm minorities and the poor more than any other group by taking away from them a very important bargaining tool to get work – offering their services for less money! The surest way to fight bigotry and prejudice in the private sector workplace is to have this ability. If an employer hates a particular subset of the society, he has to pay for that prejudice by not hiring people from that group at a lower wage. He has to pay more to employ the people he prefers, taking money out of his pockets and food off of his dinner table.

Aided by my father's revelations, I was able to understand firsthand how nothing done by a government should be judged by its stated intentions, but by its results and the damage it will cause to society.

There are those good-intentioned do-gooders who argue that raising the minimum wage increases the money in circulation, allowing people to purchase more and bolster a sagging economy. Every historical example my father gave showed that it does nothing of the sort. In fact, it does just the opposite.

So, just who benefits from these laws if economists can clearly demonstrate the harm they do to society?

The answer is politicians looking for votes among the working poor and the unskilled, who always cheer for the perceived benefits they will garner. Labor unions, whose members typically earn so far above the minimum wage that it should seem a moot issue, love the minimum wage precisely because it stops non-union workers from entering into competition with them, enabling them to keep their higher wages. You see, when they use terms like "scabs" and "unfair labor practices" what is actually meant is "people willing to work for less doing the same job at a lower cost to the consumer." It also increases what the union members could ask for in wages because, typically, their contracts are "pegged" to the minimum wage.

When the dust clears after the implementation of these mandates, the do-gooders go on to a different cause to champion, the politician gets to thump his chest and brag how he helped the poor, the unions go on gouging the consumer, and the poor stop cheering when they find their employers have either closed their doors or set up shop elsewhere and they are in the unemployment line.

As my father told me, "No politician, no economist, and no socialist democrat will ever answer the question as to how it is of benefit to you, or to society, to be unemployed at $2.00 an hour rather than to be employed at $1.85."

DR. THOMAS V. GIORDANO

My father did, however, tell me when an increase in the minimum wage is justified, it is when it is done on an individual business level. When a company or business is looking to hire the most qualified worker, or to hold on to a worker that it has trained, it is in the interest of the company to offer a higher wage than its competitors as an incentive for skilled labor to prefer that workplace. However, in these cases, the increase in the minimum wage is based upon productivity which has been analyzed by the company itself for profit reasons, not as a feel-good attempt to effect charity for the working man at the expense of the owners, the stockholders, the consumer, or the public. Across-the-board, mandated increases in wages do more damage than good in any market, whether it be open and free or not. The government should never be placed in a position to determine the value of a service to an employer; that should be mutually agreed upon between employer and employee.

CHAPTER 20

ANOTHER CLASSROOM, ANOTHER SOCIALIST

The 1973-74 school year was my last at Cherry Hill High School West. During that last year, I met an exchange student from Santiago de Chile. Her name was Luz Maria and she spoke little English. Fortunately, after having studied six years of Spanish, I was quite proficient in the language and we were able to communicate very nicely. Since we shared a few classes together, the teachers paired us off so I could translate. Luz Maria was very pretty and for me it was a stroke of luck. We gradually got to know each other well, so I eventually got up the courage to ask her out and she accepted.

She was staying with the family of another student whom I didn't know and, though they were Roman Catholic, they were not Italian. In any case, we started going out regularly on the week-ends and I would often take her to my home for dinner because she developed a great rapport with my mother. She actually preferred staying with us as much as possible because she found our two cultures very similar. I was amazed to watch my mother having discussions with her in the Calabrese dialect of Italian with Luz Maria responding in Spanish as though they were speaking the same language.

Eventually, the time came for my *polola,* the Chilean word for 'girlfriend,' to return to her home and family.

Soon after Luz Maria had returned to Santiago, we received a phone call from her and her parents. They were so pleased with the way our family treated their daughter that they wanted to reciprocate and invited me to stay my summer with them after my school year had ended. It would also give me the opportunity to meet my mother's relatives in Argentina, with a short plane trip to Buenos Aires, before returning home to start my freshman year at college.

Before my trip, my father gave me some advice on how to conduct myself. He told me to keep my eyes and ears open and my mouth shut as much as possible. He reminded me that the country was still going through some turmoil after the fall of the *Allende* government and it would be wise not to attract too much attention to myself. Most important of all, I was to respect any police or military people that I came in contact with.

It was a very long journey from Philadelphia that required three plane rides – to Miami, then to Lima, Peru, and on to Santiago de Chile. The strangest thing to me was that I hadn't even left the time zone that I started in.

UNALIENABLE

My visit to Chile opened my eyes to so many things on so many levels that it is difficult to imagine what my life from that point on would have been had I not taken up the invitation. I was introduced to their food, their culture, their history and to their amazingly beautiful country. I was also exposed to some of the most incredible Spanish guitar music I had ever heard.

In mid-August, Luz Maria's father, Señor Rigoberto, came home from work and asked me if I liked Spanish guitar music. I told him that I did and was particularly impressed by Andrès Segovia and Julian Bream. He asked me if I had ever heard Narciso Yepes play. I told him that I hadn't. He responded that he had two tickets for a performance by Yepes that was to take place at the Teatro Municipal de Santiago that week. In his opinion, it was one of the most beautiful concerts ever written for the guitar. It was an opportunity that I'm happy I didn't miss – for more reasons than one.

El Concierto de Aranjuez by Joaquìn Rodrigo, without exaggeration, was precisely as Luz Maria's father had described it. Yepes' mastery of his custom-made, ten-stringed guitar was unbelievable to behold. Though the concert itself did leave a lasting impression upon me, it was not the most significant experience that I had that evening.

Before the concert began, the orchestra and El Maestro Yepes sat patiently tuning their instruments on stage as the audience settled down and quieted themselves. Suddenly, Luz Maria elbowed me indicating that we should stand. Everyone stood in unison and applauded as

DR. THOMAS V. GIORDANO

El Generàl Augusto Pinochet Ugarte entered with his wife. They stood in front of their seats and bowed to the audience and the orchestra. I was sincerely impressed with the truly heart-felt admiration those in attendance expressed toward the General and his wife. The ovation lasted at least a minute before the General had his wife sit and gestured to Maestro Yepes on the stage to commence.

The impression that I was led to believe from the press and other media in the United States on the subject of the recent mayhem in Chile was that there was a military coup that overthrew a democratically elected president and now governed as a military junta. They reported that Allende was assassinated in a bloody takeover. They reported suppression of the people and numerous *desaparecidos*.

It was true that there was a one o'clock a.m. curfew and the streets were empty by that hour. It was also true that there were armed military practically everywhere we went in Santiago. We had been stopped at checkpoints and had our documents examined many times, but never discourteously or with an overt threat of violence. I also witnessed the damage that was still apparent near the city center and seats of governmental authority, all of which was still being repaired.

The reaction to the General prompted me wondering how the Chilean people I saw in the theater could show such a deep appreciation for a man that was supposedly just another evil dictator who wrested control from a legitimate government and deprived them of their freedoms. Did the Chileans know something that I didn't? Was I somehow misinformed about what actually happened on September 11, 1973?

Until that point in my stay, I hadn't touched on the subject of the junta out of politeness, though I did notice that Luz Maria's family seemed enthusiastic about the country's future.

One Saturday morning after the concert, Luz Maria's older brother, Germàn Alejandro, brought me to a place in the city called *Providencia*. It was a wide boulevard where every Saturday morning the youth of Santiago gather to meet each other and plan their weekends. I accompanied him on rounds meeting girls and friends, and noticed a general feeling of joyfulness – a certain cheerfulness with life. Every one of the girls I met was flirtatious and curious to meet me – a *norteamericano*. Some, after hearing me speak Spanish, didn't believe that I was from the United States and playfully asked to see my passport. They seemed just as impressed with my Italian surname as they were with my being from Philadelphia.

The Chilean youth had this custom of handing out business cards with only their names printed on them when meeting someone they didn't know. Germàn explained to me that if they wrote their phone number on it, they were asking the person they gave the card to if they wanted to go out with them. I guess I was a novelty because by the time ten o'clock came around, I had about a dozen of these cards, but could not reciprocate because I had no idea that the tradition existed. Riding home in the car, Germàn suggested that I give the cards to him so that his sister wouldn't get angry with me. In any event, what struck me was the complete, carefree attitude these kids had. I had no sense that they felt oppressed by some evil dictator. I got the distinct impression that the youth considered the check-points, the armed military presence, and the curfew as merely temporary inconveniences that were a fair trade-off for what they had experienced during Allende's aborted control over their country. In fact, they worked around the curfew by having parties from curfew to dawn, when they could safely return home.

The truth about the Allende government became clear to me over the next few weeks, especially during a long train ride from Santiago to Concepciòn, a town in the south of the country. The events of the previous four years were still fresh in the minds of everyone I spoke with. What became apparent to me was that those events were diametrically opposed to the media reports I had heard in the United States. It brought home to me the expression attributed to Mark Twain about the media: If you don't read the papers, you are uninformed; if you do read them, you are misinformed!

It became gradually apparent to me that the papers and television media had been superficially correct, as far as the names, dates and some details went, but had completely missed the boat when describing accurately the actual events of the take-down of Dr. Allende's Marxist regime. They had also conveniently omitted important key factors in those events. By the time my stay had ended and I was on my way to Argentina, my heart was aching at the thought of leaving Luz Maria and the realization that we would probably never see each other again. I did, however, have a complete picture of just what had happened in Chile and it was in full accord with my father's instructions regarding state-run economies and socialism as an applied, political theory. I understood with clarity the predictability of the failure of any system based upon theft, coercion, and the violation of the people's natural, personal, civil, and political rights.

It was mid-afternoon on a Thursday when I arrived at the Philadelphia International Airport. I was met by my two brothers and my mother. My father was not able to come to see me arrive as he was at the college preparing for the upcoming semester. However, when we finally did get home, my father was waiting for us.

We spent the rest of the afternoon and evening discussing my trip and I also filled in my mother on her family, whom she had never met, living in Avellaneda, Argentina. Though I didn't have jet lag, I was quite tired from the journey and went to bed early. The weekend was pretty uneventful, but I did get to see my buddy Frank on Friday and Saturday.

My first class at college on Monday morning was Western History. The professor was a middle-aged man and a proud holder of a Ph.D. in the subject he was teaching. He began by saying he was not going to take roll, but that he expected us to attend class. He started on his outline of what we were going to be taught and what was expected of us. After this, he went into a short description of the importance of history, as a subject, and went through a few of the recent events our country was going through. For some reason, he even mentioned the first anniversary of the overthrow of the Chilean government.

His views on the present government in Chile were not flattering and he blamed the overthrow squarely on the United States. It was when he began to praise the Allende regime for its reforms that I began to squirm in my seat. He presented those events in the exact same manner as they were referred to in the news media – superficially, unexamined, and misleading. It was his pomposity, however, and his elitist attitude that really got me.

I raised my hand and he called on me.

"Professor, you are giving the impression that the military overthrew the Allende regime in a bloody takeover with the assistance of the CIA. You've even suggested that he was assassinated. May I ask what your source for this opinion is?"

"This isn't my opinion; it is what has been reported by the primary sources."

"By primary sources, are you referring to newspaper articles and television reports?"

"Among other things."

"Other things?"

"Interviews from people who have escaped from Chile with first-hand knowledge of the events."

"Forgive me, Professor, but I believe they have a first-hand point of view of the events. What would you say if you knew that after Allende Gossens fell, no one was prevented from leaving the country if they wished to do so, that travel into and out of the country continued with no interruptions?"

"I'm not sure I understand your point."

"My point is simple: when these sources say they were escaping Chile in fear after a Marxist regime had collapsed, wouldn't it be reasonable to assume they were on the side that was overthrown and that their views on the events would have been favorable to Allende and critical of Pinochet and the junta? It appears to me the primary sources you refer to are the rats that jumped ship when it sank."

The professor, who was leaning against the front of his desk, straightened up and crossed his arms. By the look on his face, I wondered if I was about to cut my own throat in my first class on the first day of college. I sensed that I would have to be as non-confrontational as possible, if I were to continue.

"Please pardon me, Professor, but wouldn't you agree that there is always more than one side to any story?"

"Of course, I would, but you cannot ignore or deny the human rights violations of the military government that overthrew Allende. Thousands of people have been killed or gone missing. This was all sanctioned and aided by the CIA and our government."

"Professor, I could make the same statement of Allende about human rights violations. It was Allende who created a secret police force to harass his political opponents. It was Allende who suppressed the newspapers and media that criticized his government. Allende and the parties in the coalition received money from the Soviet Union through the KGB to advance their ideology in South America, in violation of Chilean law, by the way. The Allende regime turned a blind eye to the murders and other crimes of the MIR, yet I heard no complaints from the press before his regime collapsed. There is no question that we regard violations of human rights as abhorrent. This is not what we're supposed to represent as Americans. However, I find it interesting that when the Marxists do it routinely, it is merely considered by them to be a legitimate means to their ends, but when the tables turn, they cry foul and they declare the retaliations against them to be violations of their human rights."

He paused a moment and asked, "What is MIR?"

I replied in the Spanish, "*El Movimiento de Izquierda Revolucionaria*. I believe if you really analyze the situation with all of the facts, you might have a different opinion than the one you've presented."

"Well, I think I'm in a better position to evaluate what went on in Chile than you are."

He was implying to me that, because he had a Ph.D. in history, he was more qualified to determine the truth of events of which he had no actual knowledge.

After a short pause, I threw all caution to the wind and continued, "With all due respect, Professor, may I ask you if you have ever been to Chile?"

He answered, "No, I haven't."

"Would you be interested to know that I've just

returned home from Chile last Thursday after spending my entire summer there?"

The look on his face was hard to decipher, but it seemed to me that he just realized he had stepped into something he was about to regret. His pompous attitude didn't permit him to see the clues in our brief discussion that I just may have had some knowledge of the events in Chile that he didn't.

I continued, "I can tell you with complete assurance that the version we read in the papers and hear on the TV news is inaccurate, misleading, and filled with half-truths and omissions. If I may ask you, just what do you know about Dr. Salvador Allende Gossens? What I mean is, do you know who this man was?"

"Well, I know that he was duly elected as president of the country. I really don't know much more about him, personally."

"If I may, Dr. Allende was a fervent Marxist and had been since he was a young man. In fact, we know now that he was a paid informant of the KGB almost all of his adult life. He was also a co-founder of the Socialist Party in Chile. The supposed 'mark' he has left on history is that he was the first democratically elected president who campaigned on a platform of Marxist reforms. Now, they say 'democratically elected' and had a mandate from the people, but this really isn't the case."

"Why not?"

"Well, firstly, in the presidential election of 1970, Allende represented a coalition of five different leftist political parties which was named the *Unidad Popular*.

They were funded by the Soviet Union and were able to get 36% of the popular vote. This is in no way a mandate by the people because it means that a majority of 64% didn't want him. Because nobody received over 50% of the popular vote, Chilean law refers the decision to their National Congress and the two who received the highest number of votes were then voted upon by the members of the Congress. For some very odd reason, Allende was able to get the votes of the Christian Democrat Party whose members sided with the UP even though they opposed him in the popular election."

"So, what you're saying is that you don't believe his election was legitimate?"

"Not at all, Professor. It was legitimate under Chilean law. What I'm saying is that it was in no way, shape, or form a mandate by the Chilean people to enact the so-called 'Marxist reforms by peaceful means' that Allende ran on as a candidate."

"Well, don't you think the reforms were necessary to help the poor, exploited people improve their lives and get out of poverty?"

"Professor, just because some people are poor doesn't mean they're exploited. Besides, when a Marxist says 'reforms,' he is actually saying 'theft with a threat of violence from one person to give to another.' This is no mystery. Normally, socialist overthrows are done by violent means; Allende wanted to do it peacefully. Can you describe to me a way to steal a person's property and wealth *peacefully*? As far as 'helping the exploited poor improve their lives and get out of poverty,' that is just a sales pitch to try and fix their ideology in a frame of humanitarianism. Looking back on the effects of his reforms shows us that it resulted in just the opposite of what his stated intentions were."

"That's kind of a harsh assessment of what they mean by 'reforms.' It's just not fair to have a small minority own everything and leave nothing for everyone else."

"If you'll pardon me, Professor, the events in Chile which led to the take-down of Allende's regime is a perfect example of what happens when 'reforms' of the nature you are referring to lead to social chaos and economic ruin. We can have a discussion of what is and isn't fair in a theoretical sense, but theft and violence, for whatever ends, are immoral. There were land reforms going on before Allende took charge. He started nationalizing the large *latifundias* which were defined by a certain number of hectares of land. These were broken up and handed over to co-operatives of *campesinos* run by committees. Everything was just fine when his government stole from the wealthy land owners, but it never stops there. Eventually, even the *minifundias*, which were considerably smaller in size, were seized and nationalized. If these owners objected to this violation of their property rights, they were terrorized or murdered by the MIR, with the tacit approval of the Allende regime. What do you think happened?"

"Go on..."

"Well, the campesinos may well have been very good at working the land, but they knew nothing about running a business, following market demands, or getting their produce to the consumers. Their production went into a nosedive and the importation of food had to increase to compensate. This proved to be bearable for after about one year, <u>then</u> most products became scarce and their prices shot up. The most devastating socialist reform was in the mining industry in the north of the country. The government nationalized copper production, taking control of foreign companies. Their economy depended heavily upon metal and mineral exports and it collapsed quickly. Additionally, what was able to be produced was traded for imports from the Soviet Union and Cuba. I was told by many that they were importing bicycles and shoes for their precious resources. As the prices for the basic necessities increased, the government issued price-fixing dictates on thousands of goods, but because these goods were forced to be sold below their actual market value, their production rapidly stopped and the government nationalized most of the private businesses. There was not a single industry left in private hands that wasn't regulated or taxed out of existence. At the same time, Allende's Keynesian economic advisors suggested that the government mandate an increase in the wages of about 95% of the people to keep up with the steady rise in prices for products that were disappearing rapidly from the store shelves. Their central bank started printing up money like there was no tomorrow and inflation hit over 1,000%. The Chilean people were literally starving with pockets full of money. People waited for hours in lines only to find that the shelves were bare. They were lucky if they could find rice and beans to survive on. The country was unable to trade for foreign goods because their credit worthiness was extremely low. That meant no meat or milk from Argentina, no wheat or corn from the United States and Canada. All of this only took a bit more than a year to happen. It was the direct result of the *reforms* that you yourself were praising a few minutes ago. I think you would agree with me that there is nothing positive about starvation on a massive scale."

By the look on his face, he appeared to be embarrassed. His pomposity was turning sheepish.

"Well, I can certainly see how this would lead to civil unrest in the country."

"Yes, Professor. This was the economic and social environment, and the political environment was no better. You see, Allende's coalition covered the array from moderate to extremely radical leftists. At the more radical end, there were those who wanted an immediate Marxist takeover of their constitutional government. They didn't want to wait for the reforms. They believed that Allende was too slow with the reforms. The second in command of his own party wasn't content that they got into power without a bloody revolution; he wanted to see a million dead Chileans! He insisted that, in order for them to succeed with their aims, at least one million people had to be killed. This was his *humanitarian* way of resolving the crisis. Allende lost control of his coalition but when he started to usurp the powers of the Deputies of the Congress and tried to abolish the constitution and create an authoritarian dictatorship, they voted for his removal with a two-thirds majority. He refused to leave. Now, here is where things get interesting and the news gives a false impression: the military was not involved directly in the take down of Allende. It was a popular uprising and tens of thousands of citizens went to the streets and surrounded the seats of government insisting that he remove himself after the congressional vote. His response was a national TV broadcast spewing some Marxist rhetoric before blowing his own head off with an AK-47 that Fidel Castro gave him as a gift after becoming President."

"So, you're saying he was not assassinated. How can you be sure of that?"

"Because I know one of the men who found his corpse. My girlfriend's father is an economist in Santiago, but is also a volunteer *bombero* – a fireman. He was among the men who broke down Allende's office doors and found him seated at his desk between two large windows and his brains were splattered upwards on the wall with his gun between his legs. There was no way he was shot from the outside."

"So, go on…"

"After Allende's death, there was a Marxist insurgency. They were killing citizens, ambushing police and military personnel, robbing banks, and setting government buildings on fire. The country was almost at an open civil war. The National Congress voted to order the military to take control and bring back civil order. Augusto Pinochet was the last to enter into this agreement at the bidding of Admiral Merino of the Chilean Navy. Pinochet, was named by Allende himself as the Supreme Commander of the Army. At first, he was disinclined and had to be convinced of the legality of such a move on the part of the Congress. He became the President of the junta because he headed the largest of the Chilean Armed Forces. In other words, the military became involved *after* the fact. To this day, they are still fighting the insurgency. Allende was no angel and he created such hardship and misery for his people that I found no one – even people that initially supported him – that said any good came out of his administration of their country."

"And what about our country's involvement? Do you think it's right for our country and the CIA to intervene in another country's internal politics?"

"No, I don't think it's right. If it were up to me, I wouldn't get involved at all in other people's affairs, but I have asked myself if this is really the case. I mean, it wasn't Nixon who forced Marxist reforms on the Chilean people. It wasn't our country that nationalized their industry and agriculture which led to their economic collapse. Do you really think that the CIA convinced two-thirds of their deputies to pass a resolution of no confidence after three and a half years of deprivation? Can the CIA mobilize tens of thousands of Chilean citizens onto the streets of Santiago to insist that the man responsible for their misery leave their government? What I do know is, that if it is true that the CIA came in to assist the junta, it was after the fact and at their request. They needed intelligence on international groups whose activities were supporting internal factions of the far left.

These people are nothing more than vicious, murdering Marxist thugs and have absolutely no regard for human life or property. I found no Chileans who would disagree with me on this point. It seems to me that if anybody wants to reform something, this isn't the way to do it."

"So, regardless of what you've said, you believe that reforms were necessary?"

"No, I don't. If we look at the land reform in Chile, for example, it is not true that reform was even needed. It is not true that all of the land was in the hands of a few and there was nothing for everybody else. I was told that the large *latifundias* in Chile made up about 58% of the total available land. There were no laws preventing anyone in their society from selling or buying land. Some of these *haciendas* were owned by the same families for generations. Property rights were well respected under their laws. They were run efficiently and were easily able to satisfy their internal market demands. You asked me about fairness; I don't think this has anything to do with the question at hand. The better question would be whether there is a right to keep and be secure on your own property. Is it fair to have your property stolen from you because some others may not have what you have? Their immoral efforts resulted in massive failures, which the government blamed on evil capitalists and U.S. colonialism! It was a complete lie; there never was any U.S. colonialism in Chile and they had already thrown the foreign owners of the mines out of the country more than a year before the economic collapse occurred under the state's administration. The Marxists blamed their incompetence and their failures on anybody but themselves and the Chilean people saw right through it."

"Well, maybe they did do it the wrong way, but there are many people who believe that there is an uneven distribution of the wealth in the world that has to be addressed in some way."

"Well, Professor, in a free society, where property rights are respected, the distribution of resources and production is based upon human choice. Let me give you a hypothetical not related to land. Let's say we live in a country of a hundred million people and there are about ten thousand involved in the ownership of three automobile manufacturing plants. Is it unfair that these ten thousand have more of an income than the rest? Would you suggest taking what they have from them and distributing it to the other 99.9 plus million? We would all lose and no more cars would be produced. On the other hand, to make things 'fair,' would you be in favor of having a hundred million automobile manufacturers – one owned by every, single person? Can you see the consequences of this idea in the long run? To my mind, 'fairness' is simply allowing people to follow their own desires, to do with their lives as they wish. Some will win, some will lose. By trying to force equality on everybody we will get exactly what they got in Chile – we will all be equal in our empty cupboards and misery."

The professor stared silently at me for a moment. He then asked me my name and I told him. He looked down at his roll book and asked, "Are you related to Mario Giordano?"

"He's my father."

He pursed his lips and nodded, then ended the class early.

When I arrived home later that afternoon, I found my father sitting in his recliner reading, as usual. He lowered his book as I approached on my way to the kitchen.

"Tommy, your history professor came to my office this morning."

"Dad, I was really polite…"

"He said you were polite; you politely made him look foolish."

"No, Dad, he made himself look foolish. I just gave him the facts as I know them. What did he say?"

"First, he asked me if you were my son and then asked if you really were in Chile this summer. He then told me of the discussion you had with him in class."

"What did you say?"

"I said, 'That's Tommy!' He's a friend of mine and, yes, he has socialist tendencies but do me a favor, go easy on him in class. He really is a nice guy; he's just wrong. My advice to you in college is simple – don't hear everything. Just because you *can* respond to something doesn't mean you *have to* respond. I'm happy you were polite, though."

As I look back on my undergraduate years, I can honestly say that I took my father's advice on many more occasions than I can remember. My experience with Chile and the press in the U.S. made it obvious to me that there was an underlying agenda to conceal the truth of anything that proved the clearly demonstrable failures of socialism and state-controlled economies.

I followed the progress in Chile from those days on and was extremely happy to see their "Economic Miracle" after applying the economic suggestions of Dr. Milton Friedman, which came to fruition within a very short time after I had returned home. Regardless of what anyone thinks of Augusto Pinochet, it would seem that Luz Maria's family's enthusiasm for the country's future, the applause of the Chileans in the Teatro Municipal, and the cheerfulness of the youth in Providencia would eventually be well-justified.

EPILOGUE

In this book, I have concerned myself with just a few of the many lessons my father imparted to me in dealing with an understanding of liberty, economics, and government, and how he taught me the fundamental principles of self-ownership. The true concept of unalienable, along with its proper pronunciation, is the key to understanding the unique view of humanity that our forefathers used as a bedrock ideology in creating a new form of government. Over the years, ambitious, virtueless people with a warped sense of domination have occupied positions of power in our government, in our schools, and in our mass media, mutating and weakening the word's original meaning. What makes our homeland exceptional is the sacred recognition that each human being has value and that that value is only subject to our own independent moral expression of free will. As my father pointed out to me, so many years ago, there is a difference between something that "cannot be taken away" and something that is "not transferable or subject to commerce." This is not simply a matter of semantics;

it is the difference between serfdom and freedom. By gradually changing the meaning of the word and its proper pronunciation, the true intentions of our founding fathers have become lost, belittled, and subject to ridicule by those who would destroy our unique and exceptional way of life.

What I have omitted from this book, however, were Buster's lessons from his search for spiritual awareness and his studies into the religious and philosophical aspects of the human condition. The subjects of this book are merely outcroppings of a deeper understanding of the free expression of the human spirit that our Creator intended.

As was mentioned before, my father was born a Roman Catholic. This did not, however, prevent him from studying and consulting with other religions and religious figures for answers. His personal library was filled with philosophical tomes, biographies of religious figures, and tapes of lectures from every major religion of the world. Looking back, I believe he was still trying to find the answer to his father's death and how it was that he was saved from almost certain death on that Navy transport ship.

I recall asking my father what his favorite film was, and he told me, without hesitation, that it was *The Razor's Edge* with Tyrone Power. He also told me that, had he not been married and had children, he may very well have had a similar life to that of the protagonist of the film. It was his obligations to our family that brought the world to him in books, rather than his journeying to the world.

I was already living and practicing in Italy when my father was diagnosed with cancer. Taking my friend Dr. Frank Pettinelli's advice, I made arrangements to fly home. When I called to tell my father of my plans, we went into a discussion of what he should do – whether he should fight it or let nature take its course.

My response to him was, "I cannot answer that for you, Dad. This has to be your decision alone. I can only give you the technical answers and prognoses as I know them. It's going to be tough, Dad. But I have to ask you, how can you ever be sure that 'following the course of nature' doesn't also include following the advice of those whose knowledge is derived from the nature of your illness? I mean, isn't the knowledge and wisdom of the oncologists and urologists derived from nature itself? Does following nature have to mean resignation to your fate?"

He went silent for a moment. His lack of response indicated to me that he was either thinking of an answer or posing a question to himself to be investigated.

"I'll have to give this some consideration, Tommy. Right now, my first instinct is to let nature take its course and be done with it. I'll let you know when you get here."

A week later, we were sitting alone together in his living room. He had no outward, physical signs of illness other than sporadic winces from pressure to his left flank. We continued the discussion we had started the week before on the phone.

"I've given some thought to what you told me and I've

decided to fight this thing. The way I look at it, there are two considerations that I have based my decision upon. The first is that the tumors and I are part of the same nature. I was reminded of the many times that Penny came home with ticks after running around in the woods. Now, the dog and the tick are both parts of nature, but it was also within my reasoning to remove them because of their parasitic existence on my dog. I view the tumors in the same way; they too are part of nature, yet I have the awareness of the damage they are causing me and want them out. Secondly, I've asked myself the simple question, 'If I do nothing and let the illness take me without a fight, am I not, in effect, assisting in my own death and committing suicide?' I cannot go to my grave with even a doubt that I allowed my life to end without doing everything within my power to prevent it. I'm more concerned with my soul than I am my body and, since I don't know with certainty what comes after, I don't want this to be hanging over me."

I was pleased with his decision and nodded my approval. It was then we decided upon a strategy as to how to proceed, prioritizing his major complaints. We already knew that he had two different cell type tumors within the same system, but all of his symptoms were more related to the transitional cell carcinoma in his bladder than the one in his left kidney. I had already done some research in Italy on how to deal with this and, though unconventional in approach, we were able to shrink the tumor to a dimension to where it could be removed through the urethra, rather than by a resection

UNALIENABLE

or removal of the bladder itself. This, alone, resolved the majority of his chief complaints and eliminated the embarrassment of having to wear a bag to collect his urine. It gave him the mobility and independence he didn't want to lose. It also meant he didn't have to burden my mother with the unpleasant task of assisting him, something he would have rather died to avoid than experience.

The renal cell carcinoma in his kidney was a different story. The best advice we had there was to remove the kidney because of many factors and the staging. It appeared that this tumor, although basically asymptomatic, preceded that of the bladder. I explained the significance and the prognosis to my father, as far as the five-year survival rate went. Though, at the time, there didn't seem to be any spreading of the tumor, renal cell carcinomas are known for their aggressiveness. He weighed and considered the advice of his urologist and had the kidney removed.

His life for the next two-and-a-half years was relatively normal and he had very little discomfort. This, however, changed a short time after Thanksgiving in 1993. After a rapid eleven-day decline, he passed away.

It was three o'clock in the morning on the 19th of December in Italy when my brother Gary phoned me with the news of my father's death in New Jersey. I was lying in bed next to my wife when I answered the phone. My brother described my father's last moments and told me he went peacefully. I hung up the phone and covered my eyes with my forearm and began to weep uncontrollably. My wife was motionless next to me and said nothing. After a few minutes of weeping in the darkness of the bedroom, I got up and went to the bathroom to rinse my face. Knowing that I would not be able to sleep, I went into the living room and turned on the TV.

I do not know whether it was fate, coincidence, or a message but on RAI TRE, '*The Razor's Edge*' with Tyrone Power was being aired. Strangely, it was in English with Italian subtitles. As I watched this film in amazement, I was illuminated. After all of his traumas, wounds and scars, after a lifetime of wonder, questions, investigations and study, he finally had the answers he sought. The moment of his death, whether its result was oblivion, the glory of a Christian afterlife, elevation to a higher plane, or reincarnation, revealed to him the truth of his existence.

He had his answers.

My profound sense of grief was instantly lifted from me and I experienced a great euphoria and happiness for him. I also realized that I was actually grieving for myself and not for his death.

I would not have enough time to make the air trip back to America to attend his funeral. He wanted to make sure that it was a military funeral to express his love for the country and attest to the war years that defined him and cast him into his future. He also wished to be cremated, not wanting to leave any physical trace behind beyond his offspring and grandchildren.

When I was finally able to return to the U.S. a short

time later, my mother gave me a packet of books that my father had left for me. They were the accumulated works of Zecharia Sitchin, collectively known as *The Earth Chronicles*. There was a handwritten note included. It read, "*Tommy, could this be true? – Dad*"

He was giving me a task to fulfill.

www.ingramcontent.com/pod-product-compliance
Lightning Source LLC
LaVergne TN
LVHW051544070426
835507LV00021B/2397